Use of Experts in International Freshwater Disputes

AF714839

International Water Law

Editor-in-Chief

Salman M. A. Salman (IWRA)

Associate Editors

Laurence Boisson de Chazournes (*University of Geneva*)
Lilian del Castillo-Laborde (*University of Buenos Aires*)
Gabriel Eckstein (*Texas A&M University*)
Makane Moïse Mbengue (*University of Geneva*)
Alistair Rieu-Clarke (*Northumbria University*)
Kishor Uprety (*International Lawyer and Researcher*)

Volumes published in this Brill Research Perspective are listed at *brill.com/rpwl*

Use of Experts in International Freshwater Disputes

A Critical Assessment

By

Makane Moïse Mbengue
Rukmini Das

BRILL

LEIDEN | BOSTON

This paperback book edition is simultaneously published as Volume 4 (3) 2019 in *International Water Law*, DOI:10.1163/23529369-12340015.

Library of Congress Control Number: 2019951465

Typeface for the Latin, Greek, and Cyrillic scripts: "Brill". See and download: brill.com/brill-typeface.

ISBN 978-90-04-42042-7 (paperback)
ISBN 978-90-04-42043-4 (e-book)

Copyright 2019 by Makane Moïse Mbengue and Rukmini Das. Published by Koninklijke Brill NV, Leiden, The Netherlands.
Koninklijke Brill NV incorporates the imprints Brill, Brill Hes & De Graaf, Brill Nijhoff, Brill Rodopi, Brill Sense, Hotei Publishing, mentis Verlag, Verlag Ferdinand Schöningh and Wilhelm Fink Verlag.
Koninklijke Brill NV reserves the right to protect the publication against unauthorized use and to authorize dissemination by means of offprints, legitimate photocopies, microform editions, reprints, translations, and secondary information sources, such as abstracting and indexing services including databases. Requests for commercial re-use, use of parts of the publication, and/or translations must be addressed to Koninklijke Brill NV.

This book is printed on acid-free paper and produced in a sustainable manner.

Contents

To the memory of Dr. Bonaya Adhi Godana (1952–2006) in recognition of his early and great contribution to the knowledge of international water law in Africa. His seminal book entitled Africa's Shared Water Resources: Legal and Institutional Aspects of the Nile, Niger and Senegal River Systems *(1985) will remain a source of knowledge and inspiration to all those interested in water law and policy.*

Use of Experts in International Freshwater Disputes
A Critical Assessment

Makane Moïse Mbengue
Professor, Faculty of Law, University of Geneva, Switzerland
Makane.Mbengue@unige.ch

Rukmini Das
PhD candidate, Faculty of Law, University of Geneva, Switzerland
rukmini.das@mids.ch

Abstract

International disputes related to freshwater resources are increasing in number and complexity. The rising complexity is necessarily accompanied and compounded by the involvement of experts in dispute resolution. This monograph examines, through case studies of international tribunal decisions, the role and use (or absence) of experts in international freshwater disputes. Through this examination, the authors identify the good practices as well as the lacunae in expert use in disputes of this nature. The monograph goes on to suggest the best practices with respect to expert involvement and use for a more fair and efficient resolution of international water disputes.

Keywords

assessors – expert witness – Indus Waters Treaty – International Court of Justice – Permanent Court of Arbitration

© MAKANE MOÏSE MBENGUE AND RUKMINI DAS, 2019 | DOI:10.1163/9789004420434_002

Part 1: Introduction

Water, water, everywhere, nor any drop to drink.[1]

1.1 *International Water Disputes*

Given the vital importance of water to life on earth, and that only a small fraction of that water is fresh water, disputes over this scarce and valuable resource are inevitable. Disputes range from access to water and related issues such as dams and river diversion, to water pollution and harm to the environment. Rivers often form international boundaries between states, and thus they become a subject matter in boundary disputes.

States thus have varied reasons for initiating proceedings before international courts or tribunals, for breach of treaties or international legal norms, all arising out of, or related to, or affecting fresh water. These legal issues often involve questions of fact, such as the contours of a river, or the extent of its pollution, which a legal adjudicator alone may not be well-equipped to handle and resolve. Considering the pre-eminence of water for survival, effective resolution of such disputes is of paramount importance. With water becoming increasingly a scarce resource, and with the steady growth in population, disputes will continue to erupt and multiply, and the claims will get more complex and novel.[2]

1.2 *Experts in International Water Dispute Settlement*

The technical nature of international water disputes has resulted in the rise in the involvement of experts in the resolution of these disputes. Such disputes may arise out of disagreements over installations situated on or near a water body or their design, impacts on water and its quality, or the natural characteristics of the water body. These may be considered the distinguishing features of an international water dispute. As a tool to assist the adjudicator in decision-making, the need for experts has arguably increased manifold in the recent past, as has its use.

It is important to define, at the outset, what is meant by the term 'expert', in the context of this monograph. None of the rules of the decision-making bodies or other international legal instruments mentioning an 'expert' define the term. There are no widely accepted definitions of who constitutes an expert,

1 Samuel Coleridge, *The Rime of the Ancient Mariner*, 1798.

2 S. M. A. Salman, *'International Water Disputes: A New Breed of Claims, Claimants, and Settlement Institutions'*, 31:1 Water International (2006) 2–11, at 10.

or what constitutes expertise.[3] Put simply, an expert is 'one who is very skilful and well-informed in some special field'.[4] The test for expertise may, however, differ in various fields. Some domains have objective criteria for determining experts – those that can consistently exhibit superior performance for representative tasks in a domain.[5] On the other hand, it is difficult for non-experts to identify experts in some other domains, and, as a result, researchers rely on peer nominations by professionals in the same domain.[6] Though it may not be possible to have a single legal definition of an 'expert', and it is not the objective of this monograph to do so, it would be useful to have parameters in international dispute settlement for identification of expertise in various domains.

The expert is examined in this monograph in the context of subject matter expertise, which refers to insight into a particular field of study such as hydrology or environmental science. For the purposes of the discussion in this monograph, an expert is a person or group of persons, or institution or organization, whether appointed by a party to a dispute, or the court or tribunal or a combination of the two, to provide an opinion on a subject on which the expert has in-depth knowledge gained through years of study and/or experience. The expert may be acting as counsel for a party, or appearing as an expert witness or assisting the court in its decision-making. The expert may even be a judge and involved directly in decision-making. An expert on water issues is thus like any other scientific expert, but with specific knowledge applicable to water disputes.

It has been seen mostly in the context of water disputes that the issue of expert use has led to controversies and procedural innovations that have clarified or modified expert use in future disputes, both water-related and otherwise. An examination of water-related disputes before international courts and tribunals, which will follow in this monograph, demonstrates how experts have been involved in various roles in dispute resolution. Attention will also be given to those disputes where experts have ostensibly not been involved, but which could have benefited from expert involvement.

---

3 See generally K. Anders Ericsson, N. Charness, R. R. Hoffman & P. J. Feltovich (eds.), *The Cambridge Handbook of Expertise and Expert Performance* (Cambridge: Cambridge University Press, 2006); M. Young & J. Muller (eds.), *Knowledge, Expertise and the Professions* (Abingdon: Routledge, 2014).

4 'Expert', in David Guralnik (ed.), *Webster's New World Dictionary* (Houghton 1968) at 168 (cited in Ericsson et al., *id.*, at 3.

5 Ericsson, *id.*, at 3.

6 *Id.*, at 4.

1.3 *Roadmap of the Monograph*

Before providing an outline for this monograph, it is necessary to understand the scope of the case law examined in this context. In analysing 'international water disputes', this monograph looks into those disputes where at least one party is a state. Thus, it covers both inter-state[7] disputes, and those disputes involving individuals or corporations or other legal entities against a state. With respect to the subject matter scope of analysis, the disputes discussed below pertain not only to water access, navigation, quality and international boundary issues, but they also include claims for compensation when related to damage to a water body or such environment.

This monograph aims to examine these kind of disputes with the goal of determining the place and importance of experts in water disputes, their increased need (if any) and how best to use them, with an overall introduction of the topic (Part 1). A useful starting point to this objective of the monograph is an understanding of the recognition of experts and rules governing them in dispute settlement provisions of treaties and rules related to freshwater (Part 2). The case analysis, focusing on how experts were used, or highlighting their absence, is divided by forum into three categories: first, water disputes before the International Court of Justice (ICJ or 'the Court') (Part 3); water disputes resolved through inter-state arbitration (Part 4); and finally, investor–state disputes involving water resources (Part 5). This case analysis is followed by a concluding comparative examination of the necessity and importance of experts in resolving water disputes, and how best to use them in such cases (Part 6).

Part 2: Legal Provisions on the Use of Experts in Dispute Resolution

The subsequent parts of this monograph describe the legal provisions on experts in the respective statutes or rules before embarking on an analysis of the cases. This part, however, provides insight into dispute settlement provisions in water-related legal instruments and whether and how they address the use of experts. An understanding of this textual aspect of the use of experts will complement the case law analysis that is to follow. A few select treaties and rules are analysed in this part, from this perspective.

7 For the purpose of this monograph, a dispute between two sovereign states is referred to as an 'inter-state' dispute, to distinguish it from other kinds of international disputes, such as investor–state disputes. Since the scope of the monograph is restricted to international disputes, this avoids confusion with disputes within the component 'states' of a sovereign state.

2.1 *Convention on the Law of the Non-navigational Uses of International Watercourses*

The United Nations Convention on the Law of the Non-Navigational Uses of International Watercourses (Watercourses Convention)[8] is the first treaty of universal applicability governing freshwater resources. The provisions on the settlement of disputes under this Convention reflect the customary principle of peaceful settlement of disputes as codified in Articles 2(3) and 33 of the UN Charter.[9] These provisions begin with the requirement of negotiation to settle a dispute between them.[10] Failure to do so opens the door to other peaceful means such as good offices, mediation, or conciliation. After this preliminary obligation of negotiation and other recommendations, the Convention provides for submission of a dispute to arbitration or the ICJ.[11] None of these options are mandatory.[12] Rules governing arbitration under this provision are set forth in an annex to the Convention. These rules are conspicuously silent on the recourse to experts, the sole mention being under Article 8 of the annex, which requires the parties to the dispute to use all means at their disposal to enable the tribunal to call experts and receive their evidence. This seems like a missed opportunity where, following other international arbitral rules, this annex could have easily included a few provisions regarding the use of experts. In a treaty of this subject matter, especially one where a fact-finding commission is, apart from negotiation, the only obligatory means of dispute settlement (discussed below), involvement of experts at the judicial stage would indeed be useful.

Failing resolution of the dispute by negotiation, the Convention lays down a compulsory fact-finding procedure. Parties are required to establish a fact-finding commission, to be composed of one member nominated by each party concerned and a member not having the nationality of any of the parties concerned chosen by the nominated members who would serve as chairman.[13] The commission has the discretion to decide its own procedures.[14] The language of

---

8 Convention on the Law of the Non-Navigational Uses of International Watercourses, 21 May 1997, entered into force 17 August 2014, 36 *ILM* 700 (1997).

9 *Id.*, art. 33(1); see A. Tanzi & G. M. Farnelli, *'The Settlement of Disputes through Non-Judicial Means (Article 33(1)–33(9))'*, in L. Boisson de Chazournes, M. Moïse Mbengue, M. Tignino, K. Sangbana & J. Rudall (eds.), *The UN Convention on the Law of the Non-Navigational Uses of International Watercourses: A Commentary* (Oxford: Oxford University Press, 2019) 349–363, at 353.

10 Watercourses Convention, *supra* note 8, art. 33(2).

11 *Id.*

12 S. M. A. Salman, *'The United Nations Watercourses Convention Ten Years Later: Why Has Its Entry into Force Proven Difficult?'*, 32:1 Water International (2007) 1–15, at 7.

13 Watercourses Convention, *supra* note 8, art. 33(4).

14 *Id.*, art. 33(6).

the following provision clarifies that this commission is functionally similar to the expert enquiry that the ICJ may order under Article 50 of its Statute.[15] Another similarity is that while the ICJ is not bound by the findings of the experts it appoints, parties under the Watercourses Convention are required to consider this commission's findings in good faith.[16] This mechanism is thus essentially an expert enquiry outside a judicial framework.

The UN Watercourses Convention was the first, but is not the only, universal treaty governing freshwater resources. The Water Convention, adopted by the United Nations Economic Commission for Europe and confined at first to Europe, has been amended to become universally available.[17] It has two new African parties and expressions of interest from Asia and Latin America. It is thus useful to next examine the provisions of this treaty, as well as compare them with the UN Watercourses Convention.

2.2 *Water Convention*

The Convention on the Protection and Use of Transboundary Watercourses and International Lakes was adopted in Helsinki in 1992 (Water Convention).[18] The treaty aims to ensure the sustainable use of transboundary water resources by facilitating cooperation among parties. The provisions on dispute settlement in the Convention are similar in some respects, though less detailed than, those in the UN Watercourses Convention described above. Parties to the Water Convention may choose to settle their dispute 'by negotiation or by any other means of dispute settlement acceptable' to them.[19] This is more permissive than the Watercourses Convention which has negotiation as a prerequisite before trying other means of dispute settlement.

A difference from the Watercourses Convention is also visible in the treatment of arbitration and the ICJ as a means of dispute resolution. A party to the Water Convention may submit a declaration that, for a dispute not resolved in accordance with the optional means of settlement mentioned above, it accepts either arbitration or the ICJ, or both, as compulsory means of dispute

15 *Id.*, art. 33(7): 'The Parties concerned have the obligation to provide the Commission with such information as it may require and, on request, to permit the Commission to have access to their respective territory and to inspect any facilities, plant, equipment, construction or natural feature relevant for the purpose of its inquiry'.

16 *Id.*, art. 33(8).

17 United Nations Economic Commission for Europe (UNECE), Meeting of the Parties to the Convention on the Protection and Use of Transboundary Watercourses and International Lakes, 'Amendment to Articles 25 and 26 of the Convention', UN Doc ECE/MP.WAT/14 (12 January 2004) (entered into force 6 February 2013).

18 Convention on the Protection and Use of Transboundary Watercourses and International Lakes, 17 March 1992, entered into force 6 October 1996, 1936 *UNTS* 269.

19 *Id.*, art. 22(1).

settlement with another party accepting the same obligation.[20] In the event of both parties accepting both arbitration and the ICJ as compulsory, the dispute would be submitted to the ICJ unless the parties otherwise agree.[21]

The procedure for arbitration is laid out in Annex IV to the Water Convention. A tribunal constituted under the Annex has the power to establish its own rules of procedure. The tribunal may take all appropriate measures to establish the facts. To facilitate the work of the tribunal, parties to the dispute are required to enable it to call experts and receive their evidence. In this respect, we see that the procedures governing arbitration under the Water Convention are identical to the Watercourses Convention. In the same manner as in the above-mentioned Convention, the Water Convention too has merely noted the possible involvement of experts, without further developing their modalities of use. Unlike the Watercourses Convention, there is no provision, mandatory or otherwise, for a fact-finding commission. Thus, purely from an expertise perspective, the Water Convention may be said to be less developed than the Watercourses Convention on this matter.

2.3 *Indus Waters Treaty*

Apart from the two treaties of universal nature discussed above, it is important to examine a bilateral treaty on the sharing of water resources, the Indus Waters Treaty,[22] not only for the management of the largest natural irrigation channels in the world,[23] but also for the innovative multi-tier dispute resolution system that can be found in it. Later in this monograph, the practical application of these dispute resolution provisions can also be seen in a discussion of disputes that arose under this treaty.[24]

The Indus Waters Treaty is about the equitable distribution of the waters of the Indus River system between two countries. India is the upper riparian of all Indus tributaries, and the Treaty gives India certain rights over the rivers allotted to the lower riparian, Pakistan, with clear restrictions. Unlike treaties in other basins that divide rivers by flow or quantity, the Indus Treaty divides the Indus system into three eastern rivers (the Sutlej, Beas and Ravi), to which India has 'unrestricted use', and three western rivers (the Indus, Jhelum and

---

20 *Id.*, art. 22(2).

21 *Id.*, art. 22(3).

22 The Indus Waters Treaty between the Government of India, the Government of Pakistan and the International Bank for Reconstruction and Development, 19 September 1960, 419 *UNTS* 125.

23 S. M. A. Salman & K. Uprety, *'Shared Watercourses and Water Security in South Asia: Challenges of Negotiating and Enforcing Treaties'*, 3:3 Brill Research Perspectives in International Water Law (2018) 1–100, at 12.

24 See Part 4.10 in this monograph below.

Chenab), to which Pakistan has 'unrestricted use' with certain exceptions.[25] India had a duty during a transition period of 10 years to supply a certain quantum of water from the eastern rivers to Pakistan while Pakistan was carrying out the necessary construction works on the western rivers to replace its reliance on the eastern rivers. Pakistan received the flow of the western rivers, subject to India's right to use some of the water for irrigation, generation of hydroelectric power, and other designated purposes before the rivers crossed into Pakistan. India is to refrain from any interference with the waters of the western rivers, except for domestic and non-consumptive uses, and certain limited agricultural use and power generation.[26] These restrictions, and the fact that Pakistan relies heavily on the Indus and its tributaries for irrigation, necessarily gives rise to disputes.

This bilateral treaty between India and Pakistan was negotiated under the auspices of the World Bank, which is also a signatory. Chiefly negotiated by engineers from both sides, this agreement is also referred to as an 'engineer's Treaty'.[27] This is evident especially from the drafting of its dispute resolution provisions. The unique aspect of the Treaty that merits its inclusion in this list is the multi-tiered dispute resolution clause in Article IX and the cases that resulted therefrom. The first step towards resolution of a dispute arising under the Treaty is reference to the Permanent Indus Commission, constituted under Article VIII of the Treaty. The Commission is composed of experts – ordinarily one high-ranking engineer competent in the field of hydrology and water use representing each of the two countries. The first tier of dispute resolution is thus examination of the disputed issue by this Commission, which would attempt to resolve the question by agreement (Article IX (1)).

Failing resolution by the Commission, the second tier of the dispute resolution clause comes into play. A 'difference' is now said to have arisen between the commissioners, which can be dealt with in one of two ways. At the request of either Commissioner, this difference is to be resolved by a Neutral Expert, according to Annexure F, Part 2 of the Treaty, if it relates to the factual or engineering matters listed in Part 1 of Annexure F. The Neutral Expert is required to be a highly qualified engineer[28] and is appointed either jointly by the two States or, failing that, by the World Bank. Indeed, the World Bank has a very important role in implementing the dispute settlement provisions of the

---

25 Salman & Uprety, *'Shared Watercourses'*, *supra* note 23, at 15.

26 S. M. A. Salman & K. Uprety, *Conflict and Cooperation on South Asia's International Rivers: A Legal Perspective* (Alphen aan den Rijn: Kluwer Law International 2002) at 49.

27 S. C. McCaffrey, *The Law of International Watercourses*, 3rd edition (Oxford: Oxford University Press, 2019), at 270.

28 Indus Waters Treaty, *supra* note 22, Annexure F, para. 4.

Treaty, a role that is made clearer in the context of the Baglihar dispute discussed below.[29] If the difference is not among these listed issues, or the Neutral Expert informs the Commission that the difference or part thereof should be treated as a 'dispute', then a dispute is deemed to have arisen. The Commission is to report this to the two governments, either of which may now initiate dispute resolution by agreement, through the process of negotiation. If the parties agree, they may be assisted by mediation. Finally, if either or both parties are of the opinion that the dispute is unlikely to be resolved by the above means, Article IX(5) provides for a court of arbitration to be established pursuant to Annexure G to the Treaty. Annexure G envisages the appointment of a 'highly qualified engineer' to the tribunal,[30] as one among seven arbitrators.

Thus, we see the incorporation of expertise into every stage of the dispute resolution process under this treaty. Such a system of dispute settlement is not commonly seen in international legal instruments. The practical application of the role of the Neutral Expert, as well as the court of arbitration, can be seen from the disputes resolved under their aegis, examined in Part 4.10 below.

2.4 *Helsinki Rules on the Uses of the Waters of International Rivers*

Adopted by the International Law Association (ILA), the Helsinki Rules on the Uses of the Waters of International Rivers are non-binding guidelines regulating how rivers and their connected groundwaters that cross national boundaries may be used.[31] Although not binding, the Rules have become widely accepted by the international community as customary international law.[32] Several articles of the Rules are devoted to dispute resolution mechanisms. As with the Watercourses Convention, the Rules envisage diplomatic and judicial means of dispute settlement. In the event of a dispute on matters related to use of the waters of an international drainage basin, the Rules recommend that disputing states refer the question or dispute to a joint agency and that they request the agency to survey the international drainage basin and formulate plans or recommendations for the fullest and most efficient use thereof in the interests of all such states.[33] While the text of these provisions remain

29 See Part 4.10.1 of this monograph. See also, Salman & Uprety, *'Shared Watercourses'*, *supra* note 23, at 20–24.

30 Indus Waters Treaty, *supra* note 22, Annexure G, para. 4(b)(ii).

31 International Law Association, *Report of the Fifty-Second Conference* (Helsinki, 1966), at 486 [hereinafter Helsinki Rules].

32 C. B. Bourne, *'The International Law Association's Contribution to International Water Resources Law'*, 36 Natural Resources Journal (1996) 155–216, at 215; S. Bogdanović, *'The International Law Association Helsinki Rules'*, 3:4 Brill Research Perspectives in International Water Law (2018) 1–110, at 89.

33 Helsinki Rules, *supra* note 31, s. XXXI(1).

ambiguous on the composition of the joint agency, since there are no guidelines or restrictions for the parties while composing this agency, an official comment clarifies that the specialized nature of these disputes would suggest the inclusion of engineers, hydrographers and other technical experts in this agency, apart from diplomats and lawyers.[34]

If negotiations fail, the Rules recommend a commission of inquiry or an *ad hoc* conciliation commission, which would try to find a solution likely to be acceptable to the states concerned of any dispute as to their legal rights.[35] If the above steps also fail, the disputing parties should resort to a permanent arbitral tribunal or the ICJ.[36] In the event that the parties opt for arbitration, the Rules rely on the International Law Commission's Model Rules on Arbitral Procedure, 1958.[37] Unfortunately, quite similar to the sparse provisions related to experts in the Annex to the Watercourses Convention, the Model Rules too only note the tribunal's power to call upon experts at any stage of the proceedings.[38]

It is indeed surprising that the same rules that recommend dispute resolution by a joint agency that includes technical experts, would recommend such arbitral rules that all but omit to mention the involvement of experts in dispute settlement. This is especially surprising given the existence of a number of international arbitral rules that refer in far greater detail to experts in dispute settlement. Although they are described in some detail in Part 4 below, a specific set of such arbitral rules is examined below.

2.5 *Optional Rules for Arbitration of Disputes Relating to Natural Resources and/or the Environment*

The Permanent Court of Arbitration (PCA) has drafted a set of specialized arbitral rules specific to resolution of disputes relating to natural resources or the environment.[39] The Optional Rules for Arbitration of Disputes relating to Natural Resources and/or the Environment (PCA Environmental Rules) modify the general PCA Rules to the extent that they can, *inter alia*, provide for establishment of a specialized list of arbitrators having expertise in the subject

34 *Id.*, Comment to art. XXXI(1).

35 *Id.*, art. XXXIII(1).

36 *Id.*, art. XXXIV.

37 *Id.*, art. XXXV.

38 International Law Commission, Model Rules on Arbitral Procedure 1958, *Yearbook of the International Law Commission, 1958*, Vol. II, art. 18.1.

39 Permanent Court of Arbitration (PCA), Optional Rules for Arbitration of Disputes relating to Natural Resources and/or the Environment (2012), available at http://pca-cpa.org/wp-content/uploads/sites/175/2016/01/Optional-Rules-for-Arbitration-of-Disputes-Relating-to-the-Environment-and_or-Natural-Resources.pdf; accessed 1 November 2016.

matter of the dispute at hand[40] and a list of scientific and technical experts[41] who may be appointed as expert witnesses pursuant to the Rules. Parties to a dispute are free to choose arbitrators and expert witnesses from these lists, though they are not restricted to these lists.

States, international organizations, and private entities such as NGOS and multinational corporations may submit disputes to arbitration using these Rules. Parties, however, must agree to submit their dispute to the PCA Environmental Rules.[42] The Rules are referred to in treaties such as the 2003 Protocol on Civil Liability and Compensation for Damage Caused by the Transboundary Effects of Industrial Accidents on Transboundary Waters.

The hallmark of the PCA Environmental Rules is the flexibility they incorporate, as they are available for the use of all parties who have agreed to use them and for a wide range of disputes. As Article 1.1 of the Rules provides, 'the characterisation of the dispute as relating to the environment or natural resources is not necessary for jurisdiction, where all the parties have agreed to settle a specific dispute under these rules'. Flexibility thus exists not only in terms of the number and nature of the parties, but also in the characterization of the dispute. This makes the scope of the Rules in terms of subject matter even wider than the International Centre for Settlement of Investment Disputes (ICSID) Convention,[43] which is limited to investment disputes.[44] Disputes under the ICSID Convention are conducted under the auspices of the ICSID and are necessarily between states and non-state entities that are nationals of other states.

2.6 *Compliance Review Mechanisms*

International legal agreements in recent times, especially those on various environmental subject matters, envisage a mechanism for facilitating, promoting, and enforcing compliance with the commitments undertaken by the parties to these conventions or protocols. Such mechanisms for assessing the compliance by parties to the treaty with their obligations under that treaty are referred to as compliance review mechanisms. While not exactly dispute settlement in the traditional sense, precisely for this reason the compliance review mechanisms under a few treaties related to natural resources and water

40 *Id.*, art. 8(3).

41 *Id.*, art. 27(5). This list, however, does not bind the tribunal while selecting experts.

42 *Id.*, art. 1.1: 'All parties have to agree in writing that a dispute that may arise or that has arisen between them shall be referred to arbitration.'

43 Convention for the Settlement of Investment Disputes Between States and Nationals of Other States, 18 March 1965, entered into force 14 October 1966 575 *UNTS* 159.

44 L. Boisson de Chazournes, *Fresh Water in International Law* (Oxford: Oxford University Press, 2013), at 233.

provide innovative alternatives to traditional dispute resolution procedures.[45] The Aarhus Convention[46] deals with public procedural rights in environmental matters, the Kiev Protocol[47] guarantees the right to information about product emissions in the environment, while the London Protocol[48] provides standards for a right to drinking water.

Compliance committees are generally established under specific instruments to monitor compliance under that treaty or protocol. The review of a party's compliance may be triggered by a submission to the committee from another party, or from the party itself concerning its own compliance, or by referrals from the secretariat of the treaty body, or as in case of the Aarhus Convention, even from members of the public.[49] Compliance committees have the mandate to examine the merits of the case (the question of non-compliance) before them. They cannot issue binding decisions, and instead make recommendations to the parties as a whole, or to individual parties.[50] The compliance committees under these legal instruments are innovative in the sense that the members, being appointed in their personal capacity, remain independent as opposed to being state representatives. This depoliticises their work and gives them greater independence and credibility. It is pertinent to this discussion to note that the committee members are technical experts rather than lawyers or diplomats. A potential weakness, that the committee decisions cannot have the same weight as those of judicial bodies, may be viewed instead as an advantage. These compliance committees are still too often considered only in comparison to judicial organ procedures, lead-

45 Y. Lador, *'Access to Justice and Public Participation in the Water Sector: A Promising Legal Development'*, in M. Tignino & K. Sangbana (eds.), *Public Participation and Water Resources Management: Where Do We Stand in International Law? International Conference, Geneva 13 December 2013 Proceedings* (Paris: UNESCO, 2015) 147–153, at 150, available at http://www.unige.ch/droit/eau/files/8214/6539/6808/Publication_Participationdupublic.pdf; accessed 20 June 2019.

46 Convention on Access to Information, Public Participation in Decision-Making and Access to Justice in Environmental Matters, 25 June 1998, entered into force 30 October 2001, 2161 *UNTS* 447.

47 Protocol on Pollutant Release and Transfer Registers to the Convention on Access to Information, Public Participation in Decision-Making and Access to Justice in Environmental Matters, 21 May 2003, entered into force 8 October 2009, 2626 *UNTS* 119.

48 Protocol on Water and Health to the 1992 Convention on the Protection and Use of Transboundary Watercourses and International Lakes, 17 June 1999, entered into force 4 August 2005, 2331 *UNTS* 202.

49 UNECE, 'Guidance Document on the Aarhus Convention Compliance Mechanism', at 2, available at http://www.unece.org/fileadmin/DAM/env/pp/compliance/CC_GuidanceDocument.pdf; accessed 21 July 2019.

50 UNECE, 'Report of the First Meeting of the Parties, Decision I/7: Review of Compliance', UN Doc ECE/MP.PP/2/Add.8 (2004).

ing to the conclusion that they are similar to judicial bodies, but without the same capacity for action.[51] Yet they have similar procedures for determining facts and for discussing different points of view. They are composed of legal, as well as expert members, with recognized competence in the field to which the treaty or protocol relates. Thus, in essence, a compliance committee provides a non-confrontational means of avoiding disputes, with legal as well as technical expert involvement.

The above examination of a variety of dispute settlement provisions under various kinds of international legal instruments was aimed to demonstrate the different modes of involvement of experts in dispute settlement as envisaged in treaties and rules. With this background, it will be interesting to see in the following Parts how a few major international judicial fora compare to these treaty provisions, and how the use of experts has played out in practice.

Part 3: Experts in Water Disputes before the International Court of Justice

A quick reading of the existing framework on experts before the International Court of Justice reveals that both the Court and parties to a case are at liberty to appoint experts. Some provisions governing party-appointed experts can be found in the ICJ Statute[52] and Rules of the Court.[53] These legal texts also provide, though in less detail, for the Court to appoint experts. Article 50 of the Statute empowers the Court to task an individual or organization with preparing an expert report.[54] Thus the legal framework of the ICJ (consisting

51 M. Tignino, *'Quasi-Judicial Bodies'*, in C. M. Brölmann & Y. Radi (eds.), *Research Handbook on the Theory and Practice of International Law-Making* (Cheltenham: Edward Elgar Publishing, 2016) 242–261.

52 United Nations, Statute of the International Court of Justice, 26 June 1945, entered into force 24 October 1945, 3 Bevans 1179.

53 International Court of Justice (ICJ), Rules of Court, 14 April 1978, entered into forced 1 July 1978, as amended in 2005 Acts and Documents No. 6 (2007).

54 See also Rules of Court, *id.*, Article 67:

1. If the Court considers it necessary to arrange for an enquiry or an expert opinion, it shall, after hearing the parties, issue an order to this effect, defining the subject of the enquiry or expert opinion, stating the number and mode of appointment of the persons to hold the enquiry or of the experts, and laying down the procedure to be followed. Where appropriate, the Court shall require persons appointed to carry out an enquiry, or to give an expert opinion, to make a solemn declaration.
2. Every report or record of an enquiry and every expert opinion shall be communicated to the parties, which shall be given the opportunity of commenting upon it.

This provision is an amended version of Articles 57(1) and 57(2) of the 1946 Rules. The need for a solemn declaration in the last sentence of Article 67(1), as well as the new final

of its Statute and Rules) envisages two kinds of experts appearing before it – the party-appointed expert, similar to a witness, and the Court-appointed one. Assessors are a related third category, which should be considered in this context,[55] because these individuals are appointed due to their expertise in certain matters.[56] Under Article 30 of the Statute read with Article 9 of the Rules, the Court may appoint assessors to sit with it. Rule 21 provides that assessors also take part in judicial deliberations. It is worth noting from these provisions that the Court has the power to appoint assessors may of its own accord, without prior ascertainment of the views of the parties.[57] All these features distinguish an assessor from an expert appointed by the Court.

The ICJ Rules indicate the flexibility given to the Court in appointing experts of its own, requiring the Court's order arranging for an expert opinion to state the number and mode of appointment of the experts.[58] This is likely to allow the Court to adapt its requirements to the specificities of each dispute.

With respect to party-appointed experts at the ICJ, while Article 43 of the Statute provides for the Court to hear experts at oral proceedings, under Article 57 of the Rules, a party calling experts must communicate to the Court's registrar, *inter alia*, the list of experts as well as the general points to which their evidence would be directed.[59] Parties may call any experts appearing on this list, and can even add names to the list at any time during the hearing, following the procedure outlined in Rule 57, if the other party does not object or

---

phrase in Article 67(2), incorporate the Court's practice in the *Corfu Channel* case. See S. Rosenne, *Procedure in the International Court: A Commentary on the 1978 Rules of the International Court of Justice* (Leiden: Martinus Nijhoff, 1983) at 140.

55 Indeed, according to Rosenne, *id.*, at 32, the expert appointed in the *Gulf of Maine* case, to sit with the Court, was an expert in name but an assessor in practice. See also, *Western Sahara*, Advisory Opinion (Separate Opinion of Judge Petrén), [1975] ICJ Rep 104, 113; A. Riddell & B. Plant, *Evidence Before the International Court of Justice* (London: British Institute for International and Comparative Law, 2009) at 335.

56 While the Permanent Court of International Justice (PCIJ) Statute restricted the subject matter scope of assessor expertise to labour (Article 26) and transport and communications (Article 27), no such restriction is to be found in the ICJ Statute. In the absence of relevant practice, the scope of expertise of assessors can only be interpreted in the widest sense.

57 H. Thirlway, *'Article 30'*, in A. Zimmerman, C. Tomuschat & K. Oellers-Frahm (eds.), *The Statute of the International Court of Justice: A Commentary* (Oxford University Press 2006) 481–494, para. 41.

58 ICJ Rules, *supra* note 53, art. 67(1).

59 This rule corresponds to Article 49 of the 1946 Rules, though the requirement of expert nationality is an addition in the present Rules.

the Court is satisfied that this evidence is likely to prove relevant.[60] Rule 58(2) gives the Court the liberty to determine the method of examining experts, after ascertaining parties' views.[61] Moreover, the Court may arrange for attendance of an expert to give evidence at the proceedings, under Article 62(2) of the Rules.[62]

Every expert appearing in a hearing is required to make the following declaration before making any statement at the Court:

> I solemnly declare upon my honour and conscience that I will speak the truth, the whole truth and nothing but the truth, and that my statement will be in accordance with my sincere belief.[63]

The wording of this declaration is an overt indication of the requirement of honesty and sincerity in any statement that the expert makes before the Court. It encompasses two aspects of an expert's testimony – facts and opinion – and is an improvement on Article 53 of the 1946 Rules[64] and Article 58(3) of the 1972 Rules,[65] which did not contain the honesty requirement of a fact witness's declaration within the expert's declaration.[66] For *ex-curia* experts, the Rules do not provide a declaration, though there is provision for the Court to require a solemn declaration from the experts it appoints.[67] Assessors also are required to make a similarly worded declaration:

> I solemnly declare that I will perform my duties as an assessor honourably, impartially and conscientiously, and that I will faithfully observe all the provisions of the Statute and of the Rules of the Court.[68]

60 ICJ Rules, *supra* note 53, art. 63(1). This is a new provision, absent in the previous versions of the Rules.

61 This is an extensively amended version of Article 51 of the 1946 Rules, with the phrase 'method of handling the evidence and of examining any witnesses and experts' being introduced only in the 1972 iteration of the Rules.

62 Although this provision is conceptually similar to Article 54 of the 1946 Rules, it has been completely reworded, and is no longer limited to the production of evidence that the Court has called for.

63 ICJ Rules, *supra* note 53, art. 64(b).

64 ICJ, Rules of Court 1946, Acts and Documents Concerning the Organization of the Court (2nd edition, 1947).

65 ICJ, Rules of Court 1972, Acts and Documents Concerning the Organization of the Court, No. 2 (Sales No. 364).

66 Rosenne, *supra* note 54, at 137.

67 ICJ Rules, *supra* note 53, art. 67(1), an amended version of Article 57(1) and (2) of the 1946 Rules.

68 *Id.*, art. 9(5).

The Statute sets out the power of the Court to lay down conditions in the Rules for questioning of experts.[69] Experts appearing in Court can be examined by any representative of a party permitted to appear in Court, under the control of the President of the Court.[70] Judges of the Court may also question them at any time.[71] After their hearing, experts are given the opportunity to examine the transcript of their statements and correct it, if necessary, just as is the case for the parties.[72]

Disputes relating to freshwater, such as rivers or lakes, have taken various forms before the ICJ. Although very often the subject of disagreements is over international boundary demarcation, disputes have also arisen in the context of building dams over or constructing roads along rivers, and environmental damage arising therefrom. This section of the monograph examines in chronological order nine such cases from the perspective of the involvement of experts in their resolution.

3.1 *Case Concerning the Gabčíkovo-Nagymaros Project (Hungary v. Slovakia)*

The *Case Concerning the Gabčíkovo-Nagymaros Project* is the first international water dispute to be referred to, and decided by, the Court.[73] It came before the Court as a Special Agreement between Hungary and Slovakia seeking resolution of certain differences that arose between Hungary and the former Czechoslovakia regarding the implementation and the termination of the Budapest Treaty of 16 September 1977[74] on the Construction and Operation of the Gabčíkovo-Nagymaros Barrage System and on the construction and operation of the 'provisional solution'. This provisional solution involved damming up of the river Danube, which had consequences for the river water and course of navigation.

The dispute saw a large amount of pre-existing expert work for ready reference in memorials and pleadings. Hungary's delegation included professors of hydrology and biology and an engineer as advocates; professors of hydrology and a civil engineer were part of Slovakia's delegation as counsel and experts. Scientists who were part of party delegations pleaded as advocates rather than

69 ICJ Statute, *supra* note 52, art. 51.

70 ICJ Rules, *supra* note 53, art. 65, corresponding to article 53 of the 1946 Rules.

71 *Id.*

72 *Id.*, art. 71(5).

73 Salman, *'International Water Disputes'*, *supra* note 2, at 4.

74 Treaty Concerning the Construction and Operation of the Gabčíkovo-Nagymaros System of Locks, 16 September 1977, 1109 *UNTS* 211.

providing expert testimony in the oral proceedings.[75] One of the key issues in this dispute was whether Hungary was entitled to suspend and subsequently abandon the works on the Gabčíkovo-Nagymaros project for which the treaty on the construction and operation of the Gabčíkovo-Nagymaros barrage system attributed responsibility to Hungary. Hungary's stated reason for this suspension was a 'state of ecological necessity'. They argued that there would be eutrophication in the reservoir behind the dam at Gabčíkovo, the Danube would be choked with silt disturbed by the drainage of the channel through the locks, and that the flora and fauna surviving in the alluvial plain would be seriously affected by the severance of these areas from the main channel. Slovakia produced expert reports rebutting Hungary's claims. Slovakia in its counter-memorial also characterized the evidence submitted by Hungary as an 'amalgam of scientifically superficial and politically oriented assertion'.

There were contradictions in Hungary's scientific data on environmental impact assessment. According to Slovakia, the stated aim of the Ecologia and Hardi reports submitted by Hungary was economic evaluation and legal analysis, not evaluation of scientific data on environmental issues. Hungary allegedly drew the wrong conclusions from these reports. In determining whether indeed there existed such a state of necessity, the Court noted the uncertainties in Hungary's scientific evidence, which led to it declaring a state of necessity. Indeed, the Court had 'asked insistently for new scientific studies to be carried out'.[76]

The scientific material put forth by the parties was also not assessed, though the Court gave 'most careful attention to this material.'[77] However, it appears that while parties examined each other's evidence in great detail, the Court did not.[78] Its decision was not based upon any of the scientific evidence put forth by either of the parties, and it did not even comment or opine on the scientific arguments of the parties in its judgment. If the Court had found good reason not to proceed on the basis of any of the scientific evidence before it, engagement with such evidence would have explained its approach and reasons for doing so. This approach of the ICJ has been said to reflect a 'certain caution' on its part to get deeply involved in the examination or cross-examination of witnesses and experts.[79] It did not find the need to determine which of

75 ICJ, *Gabčíkovo-Nagymaros Project* (*Hungary/Slovakia*), Public sitting held on Tuesday 4 March 1997, Verbatim Record 1997/3, at 28–29.

76 *Gabčíkovo-Nagymaros Project* (*Hungary/Slovakia*), Judgment, ICJ Reports 1997, 7, at 42.

77 *Id.*

78 A. Riddell, *'Scientific Evidence in the International Court of Justice: Problems and Possibilities'*, 20 Finnish Yearbook of International Law (2009) 229–258, at 235–236.

79 P. Sands, *'Water and International Law: Science and Evidence in International Litigation'*, 22:4 Environmental Law and Management (2010) 151–161, at 153.

those points of view was scientifically better founded in order to respond to the questions put to it in the *compromis*. While noting that there was a potential environmental impact, the Court decided to base its decision on the legal obligations of the parties arising out of treaty law, and not upon any appraisal of the scientific evidence.[80] In the Court's view, it was 'not necessary in order to respond to the questions put to it in the Special Agreement for it to determine which of those points of view is scientifically better founded'. A primary reason for this was that the possible ecological damage was not 'imminent' (as required in the plea of necessity), and abandoning the project was not the only option available to Hungary.

Unlike other ICJ cases discussed in this section, no dissenting judge criticized the non-use of Article 50 of the Statute[81] in this case. Nevertheless, it is surprising why the Court did not order for an expert opinion or enquiry of its own, since it felt the need for new scientific studies. It was unusual that the Court was able to take a decision on the immediacy and gravity of the environmental danger without considering the scientific data submitted by the parties intended to prove just that.[82] In respect of the illegality of the unilateral assumption by Czechoslovakia of control of a part of the Danube, a shared resource, the Court justified its conclusion principally by reference to the law of international watercourses, with only a passing reference to the adverse environmental consequences of the seizure.[83] Court experts could have been used to help the Court in weighing and evaluating the scientific evidence produced by the parties. Without these experts, the Court has been criticized for evaluating the evidence on its own, in effect, conducting an assessment beyond its technical competence.[84] While scientists appearing as counsel avoid the need to spend time on lengthy questioning of experts, the disadvantage of experts

---

80 Riddell, *supra* note 78, at 245.

81 ICJ Statute, *supra* note 52, art. 50 (empowering the Court to task an individual or organization with preparing an expert opinion).

82 *Gabčíkovo-Nagymaros Project (Hungary/Slovakia)*, Judgment, Dissenting Opinion of Judge Herczegh, ICJ Reports 1997, 176, at 177; L. G. J. Thomson, *'The ICJ and the Case Concerning the Gabčíkovo-Nagymaros Project: The Implications for International Watercourses Law and International Environmental Law'*, 3 Centre for Energy, Petroleum, Mineral Law and Policy Annual Review (1999) Article 8.

83 P. Sands, *'Watercourses, Environment and International Court of Justice: The Gabčíkovo-Nagymaros Case'*, in S. M. A. Salman & L. Boisson de Chazournes (eds.), *International Watercourses: Enhancing Cooperation and Managing Conflict* (Washington, DC: The World Bank, 1998), 103–126, at 105.

84 D. Peat, *'The Use of Court-Appointed Experts by the International Court of Justice'*, 84:1 British Yearbook of International Law (2014) 271–303, at 285.

playing the role of counsel is that the evidence and expertise is not tested,[85] as would be done in oral examination of expert witnesses.

In the course of proceedings, the Court itself conducted a site visit (without appointing experts). Party experts (acting as counsel rather than witness) were involved in this site visit at several stages. It was decided in advance that before the visit commenced, the Court would hear brief presentations from the experts from the two sides. Three days later, brief summaries of the visit would be given by the experts, who were then available to answer any questions from members of the Court. To prevent the site visit from becoming another opportunity for oral pleadings, the delegation of each party was limited to the Agent plus three other representatives (experts), whose mandate was to give explanations of a purely technical nature. Presentations would be made by members of the presenting party's delegation and also by experts not included in the official delegation when their expertise related to a specific location. To avoid any resemblance to cross-examination, the Court could ask questions to the presenting party, while the other party could only make brief factual or technical responses to any presentation or answer, and not ask additional questions. In reality, the Court asked questions of the experts on every day of the site visit, demonstrating a keen understanding of the technical issues. The visit was deemed a success.[86]

Notwithstanding this site visit, if one were to assess the outcome of the case as a whole, its hallmark may be the sidestepping of scientific complexities,[87] and one of the primary reasons seems to be its handling or avoidance in handling scientific evidence. In spite of the Court's engagement with experts during the site visit, the judgment, where one would seek out the reasons for a judicial decision, is marked by sparse reasoning and analysis when it comes to scientific evidence. This is especially noticeable when compared to the copious amounts of scientific arguments and evidence submitted by the parties.

3.2 *Case Concerning Kasikili/Sedudu Island* (*Botswana v. Namibia*)

In the dispute over the Kasikili/Sedudu Island, Botswana and Namibia had requested the Court, by special agreement, to determine the boundary between the two countries around this island, when a joint team of technical experts was unable to do so.[88] The island, known as Kasikili in Namibia and as Sedudu in Botswana, is a riverine island lying in the Chobe River, a tribu-

85 Sands, *'Water and International Law'*, *supra* note 79, at 153.

86 P. Tomka, *'The First Site Visit of the International Court of Justice in Fulfilment of Its Judicial Function'*, 92:1 American Journal of International Law (1998) 133–140, at 136–139.

87 Sands, *'Water and International Law'*, *supra* note 79, at 155.

88 *Kasikili/Sedudu Island* (*Botswana/Namibia*), Merits, Judgment, ICJ Reports 1999, 1045, at 1049.

tary of the Zambezi, on the border between Botswana and Namibia. Before the Court, Botswana's delegation included a hydrologist, a civil engineer, and cartographers as scientific and technical advisers while Namibia's delegation included a cartographer as technical adviser. Namibia's memorial and reply also included expert reports on topics such as geomorphology.

The Court decided the case based on the interpretation of an old colonial treaty.[89] The parties each claimed the Kasikili/Sedudu Island based on their respective interpretations of the treaty, with regard to delimitation of their borders. The Court considered the depth, width, flow, and navigability of a disputed channel in order to supplement ambiguity in this treaty.[90] The German version of the treaty used the term 'thalweg' of that channel, as opposed to 'centre of the main channel' used in the English version. The Treaty did not include any criteria or provide any guidance for determining the main channel. The Court, in interpreting the meaning of the term 'thalweg', referred to the work of scholars in this area, including the Institute of International Law. It thereafter concluded that the phrase 'centre of the main channel' had the same meaning as 'thalweg des Hauptlaufes' (the last word meaning 'main channel'). In the absence of a treaty definition of the 'main channel' of the Chobe River, the case centred on the interpretation of the phrase 'main channel'. More specifically, the real dispute between the parties was regarding the location of the main channel where the international boundary lies.[91] The ICJ concluded that the deep points of navigation across the river constitute the boundary between the two countries. Drawing the borders along the deep points of navigation placed the island in the part of the Chobe River falling under the jurisdiction of Botswana.[92]

Judge Oda, in his separate opinion, expressed regret that the Court had 'made no attempt to obtain the opinion of an expert regarding the main channel of the Chobe River and relied instead on the opinions of experts who were members of the Parties' respective teams'.[93] This was an explicit step forward from the previous case, where no such suggestion was made by any of the judges. According to Judge Oda, the criteria for determining the main chan-

89 Helgoland–Zanzibar Treaty (Anglo-German Agreement), 1 July 1890, available at http://germanhistorydocs.ghi-dc.org/pdf/eng/606_Anglo-German%20Treaty_110.pdf; accessed 19 July 2019.

90 Boisson de Chazournes, *supra* note 44, at 208.

91 S. M. A. Salman, *'International Rivers as Boundaries: The Dispute over Kasikili/Sedudu Island and the Decision of the International Court of Justice'*, 25:4 Water International (2000) 580–585, at 582.

92 Salman, *'International Water Disputes'*, *supra* note 2, at 5.

93 *Kasikili/Sedudu Island (Botswana/Namibia)*, Merits, Separate Opinion of Judge Oda, ICJ Reports 1999, 1116, at 1142.

nel of the river were different from technically applying those criteria to the facts. The first may be determined by applying the law, with the assistance of scientific knowledge, but the second was clearly not a legal task. The majority had performed this task merely by relying on parties' pleadings, 'without the benefit of objective scientific knowledge, which it could have obtained itself but chose not to'.[94] Botswana, in its counter-memorial, had also suggested an expert under Article 50 for the purpose of boundary delimitation.

An interesting counterpoint can be seen in the dissenting opinion of Judge Weeramantry. He doubted whether the problem before the Court could be solved by scientific evidence. According to him, this was a question of treaty interpretation. Given that the treaty was over a century old, he emphasized the importance of applying intertemporal legal criteria, rather than modern scientific criteria:

> While not discounting the high scientific and technical expertise of the experts who have been called before the Court by both Parties, it is necessary to note that there is a limit to the assistance they can give in the determination of the question which is the main channel of the Chobe River.... If the term "main channel" had been used in a contemporary treaty, and we were seeking the true meaning of that term, scientific evidence on such matters as depth, volume, breadth, and flow would help us considerably. But the Treaty under examination is over a century old and, even if depth, volume, breadth and flow had been constant over the years, modern scientific criteria are not the indicia appropriate for determining what was commonly understood to be the main channel a hundred years ago. I hence have considerable difficulty in reaching a definitive conclusion based upon the scientific evidence in this case.... I have grave doubts that the problem before the Court can in any event be resolved by scientific evidence. The question we are faced with is the meaning of an expression used by the Parties, which meaning has to be gathered not from quantitative statistics of volume and flow and depth, but rather from the Parties' own understanding at the time of the apparently simple language used in the Treaty. This was a non-technical understanding, not dependent upon expert scientific opinion or precise quantitative data.[95]

This case is thus illustrative not only for the similarity in approach to expert use as in the previous case, but also for the interesting counterpoints presented

---

94 *Id.*, at 1119.

95 *Kasikili/Sedudu Island (Botswana/Namibia)*, Merits, Dissenting Opinion of Vice-President Weeramantry, ICJ Reports 1999, 1153, at 1157 and 1175.

by dissenting and separate opinions. While Judge Oda called on the Court to resort to expert opinion, an important exception to relying on scientific evidence may be considered from Judge Weeramantry's dissent. Per this argument, scientific evidence is not useful in interpreting the terms of a century-old treaty, although it would have been were the same treaty a contemporary one. However, it must be noted that if legal minds of today are capable of interpreting terms of an ancient treaty, contemporary scientific minds should also be able to provide an expert opinion on the technical aspects of a river channel a hundred years ago. In any case, the experts would at least be in a position to provide a definite answer on whether or not they can give such an opinion.

3.3 *Land and Maritime Boundary between Cameroon v. Nigeria*

In *Cameroon v. Nigeria*,[96] the freshwater aspect of the boundary dispute involved delimitation of borders around the area of the Lake Chad basin, as well as the maritime boundary. The Court ruled in 2002 in favour of Cameroon on the maritime boundary and in favour of Nigeria on the land and water boundaries. The decision was based on the Court's interpretation of a 1919 colonial treaty[97] that divided the colonial mandate for the Cameroons (present Cameroon and Nigeria) between France and Britain. In the case of the land and water boundaries, the Court confirmed that the frontier follows the line of the watershed of the Tsikakir River and the Mou River, as the treaty stipulated, and that would place the disputed land area under Nigeria. The Court noted further that the Lake Chad Basin Commission has been authorized by the riparian states to demarcate the boundaries in the areas not covered by agreements, and that the Commission should embark on that task.[98]

In this case, while both parties had expert cartographers, engineers, and other experts on their delegations, a great difficulty in the judgment arose from the challenges of implementing the boundary demarcated by the Court. While plotting the latitudinal and longitudinal coordinates of the boundary, the Court failed to take into account the curvature of the Earth, thus it did not define the geodetic datum on which the coordinates are based.[99] In other words, there exist multiple systems of coordinates or reference points (geodetic data) that can be used to locate places on the earth. Using one system of coordinates instead of another may shift a point on earth by a few metres or kilometres. For this reason, it is important to define the geodetic datum

---

96 *Land and Maritime Boundary between Cameroon and Nigeria* (*Cameroon v. Nigeria: Equatorial Guinea intervening*), Judgment ICJ Reports 2002, 303.

97 Franco-British Declaration (Milner-Simon Declaration), LON/BPC/MAN/75 (1919).

98 Salman, *'International Water Disputes'*, *supra* note 2, at 5.

99 Riddell & Plant, *supra* note 55, at 348.

while plotting coordinates, which the ICJ did not do. As a result, it may not be possible to accurately determine the point to which the coordinates refer, resulting in a point being plotted at a considerable distance from the intended site.[100] Scholars have commented that using an expert cartographer in such cases could ensure that the judgments draw the exact line that they describe.[101] To implement this decision, the two countries had to establish a commission, which did not have a straightforward task set out before it. This commission is yet to complete its work.[102]

The decision in the above case has been criticized for its apparent technical errors, described above, with boundary lines charted or detailed incorrectly.[103] It appears that the Court's approach here was to disregard the expert evidence presented by the parties and to draw its own conclusions on the facts that it considered relevant. It drew these conclusions without expert assistance,[104] and it is unclear from the judgment, on what reasoning these conclusions were based.

3.4 *Frontier Dispute (Benin v. Niger)*

A dispute arose between Benin and Niger, two West African nations, over their borders across the Niger River sector and on the ownership of islands in the River. The two states asked a chamber of the ICJ, constituted for this case, to determine the international boundary along the Niger River and Mekrou River sectors, which separate them, as well as sovereignty over several islands in the Niger River sector.

Niger based its claim on the theory of the deepest points of navigation in the river as constituting the boundaries. Benin, on the other hand, claimed the borders to be the eastern bank of the river, thus resulting in the river falling entirely within its territory. The ICJ chamber accepted Niger's claim that the boundary should follow the main navigable channel of the Niger River,

---

100 *Id.*

101 C. Schofield & C. Carleton, *'Technical Considerations in Law of the Sea Dispute Resolution'*, in A. G. Oude Elferink & D. R. Rothwell (eds.), *Oceans Management in the 21st Century: Institutional Frameworks and Responses* (Leiden: Martinus Nijhoff, 2004) 231–254, at 251.

102 United Nations Office for West Africa, 'Communiqué Adopted at the Thirty Second Session of the Cameroon-Nigeria Mixed Commission Established pursuant to the Geneva Joint Communiqué of 15 November 2002', Abuja, 2 February 2014, available at http://unowa.unmissions.org/sites/default/files/Communique%2032MC%20Feb14%20English%20FINAL.pdf, accessed 29 January 2019.

103 Riddell & Plant, *supra* note 55, at 348–349; J. G. Sandoval Coustasse & E. Sweeney-Samuelson, *'Adjudicating Conflicts over Resources: The ICJ's Treatment of Technical Evidence in the Pulp Mills Case'*, 3 Goettingen Journal of International Law (2011) 447–471, at 459.

104 Coustasse & Sweeney-Samuelson, *id.*, at 460.

resulting in the disputed islands falling within the jurisdiction of Niger.[105] Its ruling was based on application of a legal principle (*uti possidetis juris*) that allows administrative delimitations established during the colonial period to become international frontiers at the time of independence. Benin's delegation included a cartographer (and a historian) as counsel and experts, while Niger included a surveyor and hydrogeologist among others, who were government employees. Aside from these 'experts', no other experts were involved in any form in this dispute. It may be considered that in applying a legal principle, the chamber was not required to assess complex facts necessitating resort to expert use.

With remarkably similar facts, it is necessary to compare the ICJ chamber's approach in this case with that of the Court in *Kasikili/Sedudu*, discussed in Part 3.2 above. The chamber in this case referred to the previous judgment, noting the 'thalweg' to be the boundary in a watercourse when it is navigable, and the median line between the two banks when it is not, although the practice was not fully consistent.[106] In the present case, it was found that navigation was not possible in one section of the Mekrou due to low water level. Parties also did not provide the chamber with any documents that would enable the exact course of the thalweg of the Mekrou to be identified. In these circumstances, the chamber considered a boundary following the median line of the Mekrou to be the most satisfactory solution. Thus, the chamber in this case did not deviate from the Court's position in the *Kasikili/Sedudu* case; rather the differing factual circumstances led to the application of a different legal principle.

3.5 *Dispute Regarding Navigational and Related Rights (Costa Rica v. Nicaragua)*

In one of many ICJ cases between Costa Rica and Nicaragua, Costa Rica filed an application before the Court against Nicaragua in a dispute concerning the former state's navigational and related rights on a section of the San Juan River, the southern bank of which forms the boundary between the two states under an 1858 bilateral treaty.[107] This treaty was negotiated as a solution to escalating border tensions between the two states, and demarcated the border along the river bank such that the entire river was within Nicaragua's jurisdiction, leaving certain navigational rights to Costa Rica. In its application, Costa Rica alleged

105 Salman, *'International Water Disputes'*, *supra* note 2, at 5.

106 *Frontier Dispute (Benin/Niger)*, ICJ Reports 2005, 90, at 149, citing *Kasikili/Sedudu Island (Botswana/Namibia)*, Merits, Judgment, *supra* note 88, at 1062.

107 Treaty of Territorial Limits between Costa Rica and Nicaragua (Cañas-Jerez Treaty), 15 April 1858, available at http://www.manfut.org/cronologia/jerez.html; accessed 19 July 2019.

that Nicaragua had imposed several restrictions on the navigation of Costa Rican boats and their passengers on the San Juan River, in violation of the 1858 Treaty, which 'granted to Nicaragua sovereignty over the waters of the San Juan River, recognizing at the same time important rights to Costa Rica'.

The Court held that Nicaragua has the right to regulate activity on the river for national security reasons. Accordingly, much of the restrictions imposed by Nicaragua did not unlawfully violate Costa Rica's right of free navigation 'for the purposes of commerce.'[108] The Court did find, however, that Nicaragua went too far in requiring visas and tourist cards and by imposing fees on Costa Rican vessels.

Though completely different on facts and subject matter, with respect to the use of experts, this case has a certain similarity with the Benin/Niger frontier dispute discussed above. The Court's conclusion, briefly described above, indicates the importance given to the phrase 'for the purposes of commerce'. The experts used in this case were unrelated to water, but rather were linguistic experts, who were engaged to interpret the Spanish terms in a treaty. While such individuals are also experts,[109] in the same way as scientists are experts, they do not come within the ambit of experts on water resources that are the subject matter of this monograph.

There are two primary legal instruments governing the San Juan River and thereby the factual situation in this case: the 1858 Treaty of Limits between Costa Rica and Nicaragua[110] and the 1888 arbitral award of Grover Cleveland,[111] former President of the USA, concerning the 1858 Treaty, its interpretation, and application.[112] While the Treaty granted Nicaragua sovereign rights over the waters of the San Juan, it also established Costa Rica's navigational rights 'con objetos de comercio' (for the purposes of commerce) on the lower course of the River.[113] Nicaragua's impugned actions included the charging of fees for passengers travelling on Costa Rican vessels navigating on the San Juan River and the requirement for Costa Rican vessels to stop at Nicaraguan Army posts along the River.[114] As a result, Costa Rica alleged that such actions by Nicaragua violated

108 *Dispute regarding Navigational and Related Rights* (*Costa Rica v. Nicaragua*), Judgment, ICJ Reports 2009, 213.

109 See *Kiliç v. Turkmenistan*, Award, ICSID Case No. ARB/10/1 (2013) (recognizing a category of linguistic expert).

110 *Dispute concerning Navigational and Related Rights*, Memorial of Costa Rica, Vol. 2, at 33.

111 Award of the Arbitrator, the President of the United States, upon the validity of the Treaty of Limits of 1858 between Nicaragua and Costa Rica, Papers relating to the Foreign Relations of the United States, 3 December 1888, 456 (U.S. Government Printing Office, 1889).

112 McCaffrey, *supra* note 27, at 229–230.

113 *Dispute regarding Navigational and Related Rights*, *supra* note 108, at 229.

114 *Id.*, at 230.

Costa Rica's navigational rights on the San Juan River under the two above-mentioned legal instruments. Costa Rica's arguments hinged on the meaning and scope of the term 'con objetos de comercio'. A broad, permissive interpretation would be in favour of Costa Rica, permitting the activities that were now restricted by Nicaragua. The latter state however interpreted the Spanish phrase much more restrictively, requiring that any navigation by Costa Rica on the River should necessarily be with articles of trade, that is, Costa Rican vessels should be carrying commercial merchandise. Tourists would thus be excluded from this definition. It has thus rightly been noted that the principal focus of this case was the meaning of the phrase 'con objetos de comercio'.[115]

Essentially this implies that the outcome of the case hinged on interpretation of a phrase in a treaty. Experts were no doubt used in this context too – linguistic experts by both parties. The above description was, however, intended to indicate how scientific experts were absent and were indeed unnecessary in this dispute. Their absence was not felt.

3.6 *Pulp Mills on the River Uruguay* (*Argentina v. Uruguay*)

This landmark case on various aspects of expert use started with Argentina's application to the ICJ against Uruguay concerning the River Uruguay. Argentina's submissions involved alleged violations by Uruguay of its obligations under the Statute of the River Uruguay, a treaty signed by these two states to establish the joint machinery necessary for the optimum and rational utilization of the part of the River Uruguay constituting their international boundary. Uruguay's planned construction of pulp mills on this river were alleged to pose a threat to the river and its environment, including the quality of river water.

While it did not seem to concern the Court in the *Gabčíkovo* case in 1997, the ICJ's perspective on the use of experts as counsel rather than to testify as witnesses, had evolved by the time it heard the *Pulp Mills* case in 2009. This practice was repeated in the *Pulp Mills* case,[116] where it received strong criticism from the Court for the first time. This case, concerning the possible harm to the River Uruguay due to Uruguay's construction of pulp mills, is very important in terms of use of experts. Argentina and Uruguay submitted a large amount of scientific evidence from national technical expert bodies,[117] apart

115 McCaffrey, *supra* note 27, at 230.

116 *Pulp Mills on the River Uruguay* (*Argentina v. Uruguay*), Judgment, ICJ Reports 2010, 14.

117 See, e.g., the 2005 environmental impact assessment of the Orion Mill conducted by the National Directorate for the Environment of the Uruguayan government (DINAMA): *Id.*, at 89.

from including experts on their counsel teams,[118] who in turn contradicted one another.[119] The Court, in deciding to 'principally weigh and evaluate'[120] the data itself to ascertain the effect of the proposed pulp mills on the river environment, was faced with a wide range of scientific issues. It concluded, on every scientific issue it examined, that Argentina had not met the required burden of proof.[121] The Court's primary concern was the involvement, in the dispute, of experts as counsel rather than as expert witnesses:

> the Court would have found it more useful had they been presented by the Parties as expert witnesses under Articles 57 and 64 of the Rules of Court, instead of being included as counsel in their respective delegations.... those persons who provide evidence before the Court based on their scientific or technical knowledge and on their personal experience should testify before the Court as experts, witnesses or in some cases in both capacities, rather than counsel, so that they may be submitted to questioning by the other party as well as by the Court.[122]

As pointed out by dissenting Judges Al-Khasawneh, Simma, and Yusuf, the Court did not take recourse to Article 50 of its Statute to appoint independent experts.[123] The majority opinion also received strong criticism from several dissenting judges, who felt that 'the Court has approached it in a way that will increase doubts in the international legal community whether it, as an institution, is well-placed to tackle complex scientific questions.'[124] The belief was that independent experts appointed by the Court 'in a scientific case such as the present dispute', would provide 'the insights to make sound legal decisions',[125] and help the Court to 'gain a more profound insight into the

118 *Id.*, at 23–25.

119 *Id.*, at 72.

120 *Id.*

121 *Id.*, at 93, 96–101 (on the negative impact of a pulp mill on dissolved oxygen in the River, on algal blooms in the River caused by discharges from the mill, on increased concentration of phenolic substances in the River due to mill operations, and on the link between nonylphenols, dioxins, and furans found in the River and the pulp mills, among other Argentine claims).

122 *Id.*, at 72.

123 *Pulp Mills on the River Uruguay* (*Argentina v. Uruguay*), Judgment, Joint Dissenting Opinion of Judges Al Khasawneh and Simma, ICJ Reports 2010, 108, at 111; *Pulp Mills on the River Uruguay* (*Argentina v. Uruguay*), Judgment, Declaration of Judge Yusuf, ICJ Reports 2010, 216.

124 *Pulp Mills*, Al Khasawneh and Simma, *id.*, at 109; *Pulp Mills*, Yusuf, *id.*, at 216–220; *Pulp Mills on the River Uruguay* (*Argentina v. Uruguay*), Judgment, Dissenting Opinion of Judge *ad hoc* Vinuesa, ICJ Reports 2010, 266, at 291.

125 *Pulp Mills*, Al Khasawneh and Simma, *id.*, at 111.

scientific and technical intricacies of the evidence submitted by the Parties.'[126] Although stressing that the final task of judicial determination rests with the Court, the use of experts was contended to be imperative, in cases with complex technical facts to establish the 'verity or falsehood of the Parties' claims.'[127] On the other hand, Judge Keith in his separate opinion did not find it necessary to resort to Article 50, considering that the data presented by parties was sufficient and straightforward enough for the Court to make a determination based on the same.[128] This separate opinion indicates that what may be considered as technical or complex evidence may vary for judges – the extent of complexity of the subject matter may be subjective and depend on the background and knowledge of the judge.

The *Pulp Mills* case also brought into focus the Court's frequent use of technical experts employed temporarily as part of its internal staff.[129] They were referred to here, probably for the first time, as '*experts fantômes*' or 'phantom experts', and could be appointed from varied fields, including cartography, hydrography, geography, and linguistics.[130] However, neither their identities nor their advice and opinions are disclosed at any time.[131] Dissenting judges and commentators[132] have stressed that consultation of 'invisible' experts in such complex scientific disputes

> would deprive the Court of the above-mentioned advantages of transparency, openness, procedural fairness, and the ability for the Parties to comment upon or otherwise assist the Court in understanding the evidence before it. These are concerns based ... on the good administration of justice.[133]

126 *Pulp Mills*, Yusuf, *supra* note 123, at 216.

127 *Pulp Mills*, Al Khasawneh and Simma, *supra* note 123, at 113.

128 *Pulp Mills on the River Uruguay* (*Argentina v. Uruguay*), Judgment, Separate Opinion of Judge Keith, ICJ Reports 2010, 121, at 125–126.

129 *Pulp Mills*, Al Khasawneh and Simma, *supra* note 123, at 114; see Coustasse & Sweeney-Samuelson, *supra* note 103, at 468–469; Sir R. Jennings, *'International Lawyers and the Progressive Development of International Law'*, in J. Makarczyk (ed.), *Theory of International Law at the Threshold of the 21st Century: Essays in Honour of Krzystof Skubiszewski* (Leiden: Martinus Nijhoff, 1996) 413–424, at 416.

130 Jennings, *id.*

131 P. Couvreur, *'Le Règlement Juridictionnel'*, in Institut du Droit Economique de la Mer (ed.), *Le processus de délimitation maritime: étude d'un cas fictif. Colloque international de Monaco du 27 au 29 mars 2003* (Paris: Pedone, 2004) 349–388, at 384.

132 Riddell, *supra* note 78, at 241.

133 *Pulp Mills*, Al Khasawneh and Simma, *supra* note 123, at 114, relying on C. J. Tams, *'Article 50'*, in A. Zimmermann, C. Tomuschat & K. Oellers-Frahm (eds.), *The Statute of the International Court of Justice: A Commentary* (Oxford: Oxford University Press, 2006) 1109–1118, at 1118.

The *Pulp Mills* decision is landmark not only in directing parties towards favouring the use of expert witnesses over experts as counsel, but also in providing some indications regarding parties' opinions on characteristics that their experts should possess in order for their evidence to have greater weight.

In this case, parties assailed each other's expert reports as well as those of the International Finance Corporation (IFC) in its capacity as lender to the project that was central to the dispute. The IFC, while providing financial assistance to the pulp mill, commissioned a private consultancy specializing in environmental and industrial matters to prepare various technical reports on the planned mill and an environmental impact assessment of it. This consultancy was also engaged by the IFC to carry out environmental monitoring of the mill once it was in service.[134] These various reports constituted part of the expert evidence before the Court. According to Argentina, the weight given to such expert evidence should be determined by reference to the 'independence' of the author of the report in question who must have no personal interest in the outcome of the dispute and must not be an employee of the government. Additionally, the 'characteristics of the report itself, in particular the care with which its analysis was conducted, its completeness, the accuracy of the data used, and the clarity and coherence of the conclusions drawn from such data'[135] should also affect the weight of evidence. For Uruguay, reports prepared by party experts for the purpose of the proceedings 'should not be regarded as independent and should be treated with caution, while expert statements and evaluations issued by a competent international organization, such as the IFC, or those issued by the consultants engaged by that organization should be regarded as independent and given special weight'.[136]

In response to Judge Bennouna's question regarding the meaning of the term 'independent expert' and whether a party-appointed expert could be independent, Argentina and Uruguay had different responses. Uruguay denied that a party's expert could ever be independent. However, it had retained experts and presented their reports in Court. According to Uruguay, such expert reports were admissible in Court as evidence, only they were not to be characterized as 'independent'. 'Depending on their quality, they could be of assistance to the Court and entitled to considerable weight'.[137] In defining an 'independent expert', Uruguay was less clear. Counsel for Uruguay juxtaposed

134 *Pulp Mills*, *supra* note 116, at 38.

135 *Id.*, at 72.

136 *Id.*

137 *Id.*; see also S. Talmon, *'Article 43'*, in A. Zimmermann, C. Tomuschat & K. Oellers-Frahm (eds.), *The Statute of the International Court of Justice: A Commentary* (Oxford: Oxford University Press, 2006) 977–1038, para. 136: 'the expert's association with a party may bear upon the weight to be given to the evidence; it does not affect its admissibility'.

'independent' with 'advocate'. The explanation left open the question of whether an expert witness appearing for a party could be independent, even if undoubtedly an expert counsel could not. Argentina's response to the question is perhaps more direct, stating that 'independence is not a matter of compensation alone, it is also a question of frame of mind'. Argentina goes on to note that the 'authoritativeness of an expert's report must be determined by reference not only to the "independence" of the author but also to the characteristics of the report itself'; namely, the depth of analyses, how exhaustive the report, the appropriateness and accuracy of the data relied on in it, and the clarity and coherence of the conclusions drawn. Further, apart from providing a dictionary definition of 'expert', Argentina actually attempted to define the concept of 'independence'. This term, according to Argentina, includes two considerations – the individual's (expert's) relationship to the parties and the expert's relationship with the matters in dispute in the specific case.[138] By these parameters, Argentina concluded that apart from those that were government employees, its experts were indeed independent. (Uruguay believed that any expert retained and paid by a party is by definition not independent.) On the other hand, for Argentina, an expert who was part of the IFC process and was defending his own decision before the Court could not be considered independent. On a related note, Argentina also assailed the expertise of this same individual, contending that in light of his training as an engineer, he was not qualified to provide expert opinion on rivers or hydrology or modelling. It is important to note however that for Argentina this lack of independence and of expertise would not be an obstacle to their evidence being given due weight if they were cross-examined in Court.

Unfortunately, the Court did not take the opportunity to rule on this issue, focussing instead on the problem of experts appearing as counsel rather than testifying before it. It chose to 'principally weigh and evaluate the data, rather than the conflicting interpretations given to it by the Parties or their experts'.[139] Separate and dissenting opinions appended to this judgment also refer to 'independent experts' that the Court could have appointed under Article 50 of its Statute.[140] This seems to indicate that they consider the parties' experts not to be independent. Of course, this is likely because parties' experts were

138 Relying on J. Salmon, *Dictionnaire de droit international public* (Brussels: Emile Bruylant, 2001).

139 *Pulp Mills*, *supra* note 116, at 92.

140 *Pulp Mills*, Keith, *supra* note 128; *Pulp Mills*, Vinuesa, *supra* note 124); *Pulp Mills*, Al Khasawneh and Simma, *supra* note 123.

appearing as counsel. Judge Greenwood in fact emphasized that experts testifying before the Court owe a duty to the Court, implying that expert counsel do not.

The *Pulp Mills* decision is, thus, a turning point with respect to the involvement of scientific experts in a dispute before the ICJ. Several important lessons can be learnt from the case proceedings, judgment, and separate and dissenting opinions. The use of experts by parties as expert witnesses rather than as counsel is firmly entrenched after this case. The practice of 'phantom experts' came to the forefront of discussions on experts, though by its very nature, the extent of the practice at present cannot be ascertained. Finally, even though a definitive answer is not available from this case, a number of interesting perspectives on independence of experts may be found through party arguments and judicial opinions.

3.7 *Frontier Dispute (Burkina Faso/Niger)*

Yet another case regarding boundary delimitation arose between two African nations, Burkina Faso and Niger.[141] As is common in such disputes, demarcation of this boundary involved drawing a line through a watercourse, the River Sirba. Similar to a few earlier cases before the ICJ, in *Burkina Faso/Niger*, even though parties had their own experts,[142] they requested in their *compromis* that the Court nominate experts for the demarcation of their boundary. The Court did so, by way of an order, clarifying that as a post-judgment step, this was not an appointment under Article 50 of the Court's Statute.[143] The Court interpreted the task of these experts as implementing the judgment, rather than assisting the Court in arriving at its decision. Here it is helpful to note that the parties in Article 7 of their Special Agreement requested the Court 'to nominate, in its Judgment, three experts to assist them as necessary in the demarcation'.[144] The post-judgment appointment of experts in *Burkina Faso/Niger* is an exercise of a different power of the Court and is not governed by Article 50 of the Statute and thus does not bring into play Article 67 of the Rules either. How these experts were appointed, and based on what criteria, is unclear.

141 *Frontier Dispute (Burkina Faso/Niger)*, Judgment, ICJ Reports 2013, 44.

142 The Burkina Faso delegation included a surveying engineer and geomatics expert, among others, as advisers; the Niger delegation included government surveyors as experts.

143 *Frontier Dispute (Burkina Faso/Niger)*, Order of 12 July 2013, ICJ Reports 2013, 226.

144 *Frontier Dispute*, *supra* note 143, at 92.

3.8 *Construction of a Road in Costa Rica along the San Juan River (Nicaragua v. Costa Rica) and Certain Activities Carried Out by Nicaragua in the Border Area (Costa Rica v. Nicaragua)*

In the *Construction of a Road* and *Certain Activities* cases, Nicaragua contended that the construction of a road by Costa Rica along the San Juan River had resulted in significant transboundary harm. Costa Rica, on the other hand claimed that Nicaragua's dredging activities had harmed Ramsar wetlands around the same river.[145] Both parties alleged that the other had breached its obligation to conduct an environment impact assessment. This is unlike the earlier *Pulp Mills* case, which saw no counterclaims, and where only one party (Argentina) placed an obligation of environment impact assessment on the other (Uruguay).

The parties' experts who had submitted reports with the pleadings were examined during the oral hearings. The ICJ, after examining 'the evidence in the case file, including the reports submitted and testimony given by experts called by both parties',[146] ruled that the dredging programme was not such as to give rise to a risk of significant transboundary harm. Nicaragua had (belatedly) suggested, both before and during the hearings, that the Court appoint a neutral expert under Articles 66 and 67 of the Rules.[147] Costa Rica objected, arguing that there was 'no basis for the Court to exercise its power to appoint an expert'. The Court concluded that '[i]n view of Nicaragua's failure to prove that significant harm was caused, the Court does not need to consider the appointment of an expert or committee to evaluate the extent of harm and the chain of causation, as Nicaragua suggests'.[148] It is significant that the Court did not find the need to use expert advice to ascertain whether significant harm was caused.

An expert report annexed to Nicaragua's memorial in the *Construction of a Road* case followed a similar structure to the reports in previous cases. However, in addition to methodology and results, the report included a detailed literature review. The introduction to the report also provided author biographies in great detail. Furthermore, comprehensive author curriculum vitae were included as an appendix to the report. A report in Costa Rica's counter-memorial was presented in the same format (Annex 10).

In Costa Rica's counter-memorial, yet another expert report (Annex 9) included not only the expert's qualifications, but also his terms for reference

145 *Certain Activities Carried Out by Nicaragua in the Border Area* (*Costa Rica v. Nicaragua*) *and Construction of a Road in Costa Rica along the San Juan River* (*Nicaragua v. Costa Rica*), Judgment, ICJ Reports 2015, 665, 694.

146 *Id.*, at 707.

147 *Id.*, at 676.

148 *Id.*, at 739.

for this report. This was followed by the methodology, analysis and his conclusions. Finally, the report ends with a 'statement of independence and truth' where the expert asserts that the opinions expressed therein are his 'true and complete professional opinion' and within his area of expertise. He drew the attention of the Court to matters within his knowledge that may adversely affect his opinion. He also emphasized his overriding duty to the Court. On the point of independence, he noted that he was not aware of any conflict of interest that might impact his ability to provide an 'independent expert opinion' and the absence of any arrangement where the amount or payment of his fees would depend on the outcome of the proceedings. Without forming an independent view, he had also not included anything suggested by others, including those instructing him. This statement of independence was reiterated in the same expert's additional report appended to Costa Rica's rejoinder, as well as some other (not all) expert reports in the rejoinder. Most expert reports include detailed curriculum vitae of the authors in any case.

Expert reports annexed to the reply of Nicaragua sometimes contained author biographies, and most of them included detailed curriculum vitae. At the same time, some reports included neither. Reports from government or government-related agencies did not contain statements of independence and often not much detail about authors. In these two written rounds where parties exchanged memorials and replies, experts responded in writing to each other's reports.

By letter dated 5 December 2014, the ICJ Registrar informed the parties that the Court would find it useful if, during the hearings, they could call the experts whose reports were annexed to the written pleadings, and also asked parties for suggestions as to the procedure to follow for the examination of those experts.[149] This is in consonance with the Rules of Court which requires ascertainment of the views of parties on questions of procedure, with specific reference to the method of examining experts.[150] The parties were also invited to indicate their positions on the allocation of time for the cross-examination and re-examination of the experts. Given that the parties did not agree fully on this matter, the Court decided on the maximum time to be allocated for examination. The parties agreed on the order in which they wished to present their experts, and the amount of time they intended to reserve for the cross-examination of each of the experts called by the other party. On that basis, the Court thereafter communicated its decision relating to examination of experts

149 *Certain Activities Carried Out by Nicaragua in the Border Area* (*Costa Rica v. Nicaragua*) *and Construction of a Road in Costa Rica along the San Juan River* (*Nicaragua v. Costa Rica*), *Verbatim Record 2015/2*, at 5.

150 ICJ Rules, *supra* note 53, art. 58(2) read with art. 31.

by a letter sent to parties.[151] This required parties to transmit the names and written statements of experts they intended to call at oral proceedings. These statements were to serve as the examination-in-chief.[152]

At the oral hearings, the party calling the expert would only ask the expert to confirm his written statement, which would complete the examination-in-chief.[153] This was a departure from the procedure followed in earlier cases, where, notwithstanding the written statements, oral proceedings had yet another public examination-in-chief prior to the cross-examination. The time allocated for cross-examination and re-examination were also different – 40 minutes for one case and 100 minutes for the other.[154] However, these seem to depend on the nature and complexity of the dispute and an assessment by the Court of the time required. The other party to the dispute would then be given an opportunity to cross-examine the expert for a predetermined period. The scope of the cross-examination would be confined to written and oral statements already made by any of the experts. The party calling the expert would then be asked by the President of the Court if it wished to re-examine him. The attention of the parties was drawn to the fact that any such re-examination could not exceed a certain allotted time and would be limited in scope to issues already dealt with in cross-examination. Thereafter, judges could put questions to experts.[155]

In these proceedings, it is important to note that the procedures governing experts were established through a combination of letters exchanged between the Court and parties, and by oral statements of the President of the Court in open court. No formal orders were issued in either of the disputes.

Thus, one can witness considerable progress in terms of oral examination between the earlier cases discussed in this section and this more recent one. While the essence of the procedure remains the same, these joined cases have seen an effort to structure the process by making it more detailed. However, these detailed procedures were still not in the form of written practice directions or even an order of the Court, but through exchanged letters and verbal statements in Court.

The more recent judgments also demonstrate that with the right procedural tools, it is possible to build capacity for judges without formal scientific

151 *Costa Rica v. Nicaragua and Nicaragua v. Costa Rica, supra* note 145, at 678.

152 (*Costa Rica v. Nicaragua*) *and* (*Nicaragua v. Costa Rica*), Verbatim Record 2015/2, *supra* note 149, at 6.

153 *Id.*

154 *Certain Activities Carried Out by Nicaragua in the Border Area* (*Costa Rica v. Nicaragua*) *and Construction of a Road in Costa Rica along the San Juan River* (*Nicaragua v. Costa Rica*), *Verbatim Record 2015/3*, at 13.

155 *Id.*

training to take decisions involving science, rather than simply deferring to expert opinion. Cross-examination aided in putting the scientific information into a form appropriate for legal application. Foster has noted that

> [t]he challenge in many cases is not to determine what constitutes good or reliable science, but to reach a well-informed view of the existing science and the boundaries of the relevant scientific knowledge sufficient to assess whether there has been compliance with applicable international legal obligations.[156]

This 'well-informed view' could come from a thorough examination of party-appointed experts in oral proceedings. It is important to contrast these procedures with those employed in the *Pulp Mills* case to note the progress in expert examination, not least due to the Court's pronouncement against expert counsel in the earlier case.

3.8.1 Certain Activities (Compensation Phase)

In 2018, the ICJ issued a landmark decision with respect to the environment. While the question of compensation is not strictly a water-related issue, the need for compensation arose out of damage caused to wetlands and water channels. Its importance in the context of international freshwater became apparent in the above-mentioned dispute between Nicaragua and Costa Rica.[157] The claim for environmental damage arose from Nicaragua's activities in excavating water channels for navigational purposes, which included removal of trees and vegetation.

This was the first time that the ICJ had to decide on, and did decide to, award compensation for environmental damage. The manner in which it went about doing so, however, leaves us with more questions than answers.[158] The reasoning in the Court's judgment is unlikely to provide much guidance for the future, in terms of the methodology adopted in valuing environmental damage.[159] The two parties had put forth very different methodologies for valuation in their respective pleadings. While Nicaragua suggested a 'replacement

156 C. E. Foster, *Science and the Precautionary Principle in International Courts and Tribunals: Expert Evidence, Burden of Proof and Finality* (Cambridge: Cambridge University Press, 2011) at 12.

157 *Certain Activities Carried out by Nicaragua in the Border Area* (*Costa Rica v. Nicaragua*), *Compensation Owed by the Republic of Nicaragua to the Republic of Costa Rica*, 2 February 2018, ICJ General List No. 150.

158 J. Rudall, '*Certain Activities Carried Out by Nicaragua in the Border Area* (*Costa Rica v. Nicaragua*)', 112:2 American Journal of International Law 288–294.

159 *Id.*

costs approach', Costa Rica's was an 'ecosystem services approach'. The amount of compensation owed thus varied from $188,504 (for Nicaragua, the party that owed the compensation) to $6.71 million (for Costa Rica). Both these methodologies had been used before. Nicaragua found support for the 'replacement costs approach' in the method most frequently used by the UN Compensation Commission for valuing environmental damage in the first Gulf War. Costa Rica's 'ecosystem services approach' reflected international[160] and domestic practice.

The Court noted the existence of other valuation methods apart from these two methodologies that had been used in the past in various contexts. Consequently, the Court decided not to choose between either proposed valuation method, but 'wherever certain elements of either method offer a reasonable basis for valuation', the Court would nonetheless take them into account. Eventually, it called its own approach the 'overall valuation approach.' Using this approach, compensation is calculated based on an overall evaluation of the impairment or loss of environmental goods and services, rather than by calculating the value of specific categories of environmental goods and services, as well as the time it may take each to recover or regenerate.[161] The Court's stated reasons for using this methodology are threefold. First, it wanted to account for the correlation between Nicaragua's activities and the harm they caused to certain goods and services. Second, because the area affected was a wetland protected under the Ramsar Convention, with closely linked environmental goods and services, this method appeared to be more appropriate. Third, an overall valuation allowed the Court to take into account the capacity of the damaged area for natural regeneration. However, these stated reasons do not clarify why this particular methodology serves these aims better than other methodologies considered. As one commentator notes, one can only assume that the Court deemed the other methodologies to be over- or under-inclusive.[162]

While the Court's judgment remains a landmark one, and indeed innovative in awarding compensation for damage to the environment, it is also marked by its opaque methodological choices and internal contradictions. The eventual amount of compensation awarded was only 5 per cent of the amount claimed by Costa Rica. Without a more detailed account of its methodology

---

160 United Nations Environment Programme (UNEP), 'Guidelines for the Development of Domestic Legislation of Liability, Response Action and Compensation for Damage Cause by Activities Dangerous to the Environment', Governing Council of UNEP, Decision SS.XI/5, Part B (26 February 2010); Conference of the Parties to the Convention on Biological Diversity, Decision XII/14 (2014).

161 McCaffrey, *supra* note 27, at 241.

162 Rudall, *supra* note 158, at 290.

for evaluating environmental damage, it is difficult to assess whether the Court was justified in awarding this reduced amount.[163]

> Indeed, it is far from clear how an international tribunal might calculate environmental damage in future cases based on this decision by the ICJ. While it may seem appropriate to adopt a flexible approach to the calculation of compensation, leaving room to tailor a methodology to the circumstances of a given case, the Court unfortunately did not adequately explain the particulars of the methodology it used.[164]

The possibility of the use of phantom experts arises in this situation as well. This opacity makes it very difficult to critically assess the application of the methodology that the Court adopted, and it provides no authoritative guidance for other international courts or tribunals dealing with similar issues.[165]

To a considerable extent, these problems could have been alleviated if the ICJ had considered consulting experts under Article 50 of its Statute. A comparison with the ICJ's earliest decided case, the *Corfu Channel* case, shows that the Court is completely within its powers and did not shy away from appointing experts to calculate the amount of compensation due. Although that was not an environmental dispute, the technical nature of valuation remains unchanged. The Court in that case appointed experts in the compensation phase to assess the amount of compensation due to the United Kingdom for damage caused to its warships.[166] The Court provided its reason for expert appointment thus: 'estimates and figures submitted by the Government of the United Kingdom raise questions of a technical nature which calls for the application of Article 50'. It is important to take note of this phrase 'questions of a technical nature' that is equally applicable in an environmental dispute. It provides some insight into the Court's rationale for using experts in this instance. Moreover, in the context of calculating damages, or indeed, in case of any scientific argument where parties' experts put forth conflicting methodologies, and if the Court chooses to opt for a third methodology, due process requires that the Court communicate its proposed course of action to the parties and invite their comments or further submissions.[167]

---

163 *Id.*, at 291.

164 *Id.*, at 292.

165 *Id.*, at 292.

166 *Corfu Channel* (*United Kingdom v. Albania*), Order of 17 December 1948, ICJ Reports 1948, 124; *Corfu Channel* (*United Kingdom v. Albania*), Order of 19 November 1949, ICJ Reports 1949 237.

167 S. J. Lamb, S. M. Pape & L. Hamzi, *'Procedural Issues'*, in J. A. Trenor (ed.), *The Guide to Damages in International Arbitration*, 2nd edition (London: Global Arbitration

The ICJ's judgment on environmental compensation that was not entirely clearly reasoned, as well as subsequent scholarly criticism of its decision, indicates that the Court would not have been remiss in appointing experts to assist them in their task. Given the Court's use of a novel approach to valuation of environmental compensation, a method suggested by neither of the parties, one may also speculate that phantom experts were used during the compensation phase of the *Construction of a Road* case.

3.9 *Dispute over the Status and Use of the Waters of the Silala (Chile v. Bolivia)*

In 2016 Chile brought a new dispute[168] with its neighbour, Bolivia, to the ICJ, this time concerning transboundary water resources. The present case concerns the status and use of the waters of the Silala, a river system the main branch of which rises in Bolivia, flows downstream crossing the border between the two countries and joins the River San Pedro de Inacaliri in Chile. In brief, the two states disagree on questions of fact and law in relation to those waters. On the one hand, Chile claims that the Silala waters constitute an international watercourse, thus advocating an equitable and reasonable use of those waters based on customary international law. On the other hand, Bolivia maintains that the water basin originates completely in its territory, thus it is not a transboundary watercourse, and that it was unduly diverted by Chile, leading to its assertion of total control over it.[169]

The innovative feature of this case lies in the prominent role played by the law on the use of international rivers for non-navigational purposes. However, this legal aspect is not relevant for the purpose of our discussion in this monograph.

The Silala water system rises from groundwater springs located high in the Bolivian mountains and a few kilometres northeast of the Chile–Bolivia international boundary.[170] Most of the springs are drained by a series of man-made channels on Bolivian territory and join to form a principal canal that then crosses into Chile and connects with other rivers to form a tributary of the Loa

Review, 2016) 107–122; see also, ICSID, *Occidental Petroleum Corporation and Occidental Exploration and Production Company v. Republic of Ecuador*, ICSID Case No. ARB/06/11 (5 October 2012); ICSID, *LG & E Capital Corp and LG & E International Inc v. Argentine Republic*, ICSID Case No. ARB/02/1 (25 July 2007), para. 89.

168 For the earlier dispute between these states before the ICJ see *Obligation to Negotiate Access to the Pacific Ocean (Bolivia v. Chile)*, Merits, Judgment, 1 October 2018, ICJ General List No. 153.

169 See Chile's application in the *Dispute over the Status and Use of the Waters of the Silala (Chile v. Bolivia)*, 6 June 2016.

170 *Id.*

River.[171] The artificial channels carrying the water into Chile were constructed in 1908 by a Chilean mining corporation under a concession granted by Bolivia.[172] Chile's request to the Court to declare that the Silala River system is in fact and in law an international watercourse governed by customary international law' would entitle it to a reasonable and equitable share of the waters. Specifically, Chile contends that the Silala crosses the border from Bolivia to Chile naturally as a result of gravity, that the artificial channels did not alter its natural flow, and that it is therefore 'international'.[173] Bolivia counters that the Silala is not a river, but is rather in the form of a number of springs on the ground that originate in its territory. The waters of the Silala springs are then artificially transported into Chile as a result of man-made changes to their natural course by way of canalization.[174] If this argument is accepted, then the Silala does not qualify as an 'international watercourse' and Chile has no right to use its waters without Bolivia's consent and without paying it compensation.

While there may be legal criteria to determine what an international watercourse is,[175] and that may be a fascinating enquiry on its own, at least one party's actions amply indicate that there is scope for expert opinion on the subject and that there may be a scientific answer to this question. Indeed, it appears that in preparation for the counter-memorial and rejoinder, Bolivia has already conducted site visits with technical experts on Bolivian soil to bolster its arguments concerning the nature of the Silala.[176]

The dispute is still in early stages before the ICJ, and it will be interesting to see if the Court takes a legal or fact-based route to resolving the primary issue in dispute. If the latter, then the use of experts will also be keenly followed in light of recent instances of expert use both at the Court and elsewhere.

From the perspective of international water disputes, the ICJ offers ample opportunity to critically examine the use of experts in disputes of this nature. The decision of the Court to appoint experts, the way parties have involved experts in their submissions, the Court's approach to the same, as well as oral procedures governing these experts – there are lessons to learn from the ICJ in

171 T. Meshel, *'What's in a Name? The Silala Waters and the Applicability of International Watercourse Law'*, 39 Questions of International Law (2017) 5–22, available at http://www.qil-qdi.org/whats-name-silala-waters-applicability-international-watercourse-law/; accessed 18 June 2019.

172 *Id.*

173 *Id.*, paras. 2, 12–13, 15–16, 21, 44.

174 Chile's Application, *supra* note 169, paras. 23–25, 32.

175 Meshel, *supra* note 171.

176 See Bolivian Thoughts, 'Bolivian Team Presents Study on The Origin of Silala Waters' (14 February 2018), available at http://bolivianthoughts.com/2018/02/16/bolivian-team-presents-study-on-the-origin-of-silala-waters-chile-to-face-a-defeat-and-ridicule/; accessed 20 June 2019.

all these aspects of expert use. A detailed assessment of the use of experts at the ICJ in disputes related to freshwater, as well as in comparison with disputes in other fora, is presented in Part 6 of this monograph.

Part 4: Water Disputes Resolved through Inter-state Arbitration

Over the past century, disputes involving water resources have been submitted to arbitration on several occasions, sometimes *ad hoc*, and sometimes under the aegis of an institution such as the Permanent Court of Arbitration. Thus, various *ad hoc* and institutional rules apply to the disputes under discussion below. Some common threads can nevertheless be found in these diverse procedural rules, particularly in relation to the use of experts. These rules uniformly illustrate the option for party-appointed and tribunal-appointed experts.[177] The PCA Arbitration Rules do not set any restrictions on the qualifications of arbitrators.[178] This means that a non-legal expert could potentially be a part of the tribunal.

The UNCITRAL Arbitration Rules concerning the form of appointment provide some indication of the independence and impartiality required from a tribunal-appointed expert. An expert appointed by the tribunal is required to submit a description of his or her qualifications and a statement of impartiality and independence to the tribunal and parties before accepting appointment.[179] Parties then have the opportunity to object to the expert's qualifications, independence or impartiality, based on which the tribunal can take a decision.[180] This objection is only possible after an expert is appointed if it is for reasons that the party becomes aware after the appointment.[181] Identical provisions are found in the PCA Arbitration Rules.[182] The requirement of independence

177 United Nations Commission on International Trade Law (UNCITRAL), UNCITRAL Arbitration Rules 2013, UN Doc A/RES/68/109 (16 December 2013), arts. 17, 27–29; see also, UNCITRAL, 'UNCITRAL Notes on Organizing Arbitral Proceedings' (2012), available at http://www.uncitral.org/pdf/english/texts/arbitration/arb-notes/arb-notes-e.pdf; accessed 30 January 2019, Note 15, para. 92; PCA Arbitration Rules 2012, available at http://pca-cpa.org/wp-content/uploads/sites/6/2015/11/PCA-Arbitration-Rules-2012.pdf; accessed 1 November 2016, arts. 17, 27–29; see also PCA Optional Rules for Fact-Finding Commissions of Inquiry 2012, available at http://pca-cpa.org/wp-content/uploads/sites/6/2016/01/Permanent-Court-of-Arbitration-Optional-Rules-for-Fact-finding-Commissions-of-Inquiry.pdf; accessed 1 November 2016, art. 12.

178 PCA Arbitration Rules, *id.*, arts. 7–16.

179 UNCITRAL Arbitration Rules, *supra* note 177, art. 29(2).

180 *Id.*

181 *Id.*

182 PCA Arbitration Rules, *supra* note 177, art. 29(2).

or other ethical obligations of a party-appointed expert is conspicuously absent in these rules.

Under the 2013 UNCITRAL Rules and 2012 PCA Arbitration Rules, the tribunal can hear experts (referred to as 'expert witnesses') at oral proceedings under the terms and conditions set by the tribunal.[183] Experts may even be heard through means of telecommunication such as videoconferencing, if the tribunal so desires.[184] The tribunal 'may require the retirement' of any expert during the testimony of other experts.[185] Parties are given the opportunity to comment in writing on the tribunal-appointed expert's report, and to examine any document that the expert relied on in the report.[186] These experts may also be examined at a hearing if a party so requests. Such a hearing may include party-appointed experts brought in to testify on matters at issue. General provisions on hearings apply in this context as well.[187]

The first seven cases examined here were decided in the first half of the twentieth century, and thus, apart from the award, not much material or information is available on how proceedings were conducted. It is nevertheless instructive to have a background of how these cases were decided before proceeding into the twenty-first century.

4.1 *Chamizal Arbitration* (*Mexico/United States of America*)

The *Chamizal* arbitration between Mexico and the United States was initiated due to a boundary dispute involving a river. In the Treaty of Guadalupe Hidalgo[188] and the Treaty of 1884[189] Mexico and the United States agreed on an international border. Under the treaties, the boundary follows the deepest channel of the Rio Grande, regardless of any changes in the course of the river. The 1884 Treaty, however, specified that the boundary would only follow changes in the river course that are attributable to accretion and not to avulsion. In the 1850s and 1860s the river migrated south, and in 1874 a large strip of land existed between the original riverbed and the current riverbed. The United States and Mexico disagreed about whether the change had been

183 UNCITRAL Arbitration Rules, *supra* note 177, art. 28(2); PCA Arbitration Rules, *id.*, art. 28(2).
184 UNCITRAL Arbitration Rules, *id.*, art. 28(4); PCA Arbitration Rules, *id.*, art. 28(4).
185 UNCITRAL Arbitration Rules, *id.*, art. 28(3); PCA Arbitration Rules, *id.*, art. 28(3).
186 UNCITRAL Arbitration Rules, *id.*, art. 29(4); PCA Arbitration Rules, *id.*, art. 29(4).
187 UNCITRAL Arbitration Rules, *id.*, art. 29(5); PCA Arbitration Rules, *id.*, art. 29(5).
188 Treaty of Peace, Friendship, Limits and Settlement between the United States of America and the Mexican Republic (Treaty of Guadalupe Hidalgo), 2 February 1848, 9 Bevans 791.
189 Convention between the United States of America and the United States of Mexico Touching the International Boundary Line where it follows the Bed of the Rio Grande and the Rio Colorado, 12 November 1884, 24 Stat 1011; Treaty Series 226.

gradual enough for the international boundary to have shifted with the river. In 1910, the two states submitted to arbitration to settle the dispute. The arbitral tribunal recommended a boundary on the line where the riverbed had been in 1864, just prior to the most drastic shift in the riverbed.[190]

A close reading of the award indicates that expertise was indeed involved in rendering the award. While the award does not mention recourse to expert advice or enquiries, it is important to note the composition of the tribunal. While the tribunal president was a qualified lawyer and professor of international law, the American member of the tribunal was a retired army general and a member of the American geographical society. The Mexican member was, among other things, a civil engineer. Thus, it may be said that expertise was built into the tribunal composition.[191] This case is one of the early examples of using technical expertise in judicial decision-making in a dispute relating to international watercourses.

4.2 *Tacna–Arica Case* (*Chile v. Peru*)

The Treaty of Ancón, signed by Chile and Peru in 1883,[192] described the northern boundary between the two states as 'the river Sama from its source in the Cordilleras on the frontier of Bolivia to its mouth at the sea'. A land dispute arose, however, because the Sama River does not have its source in the Cordilleras on the frontier of Bolivia, and thus it was unclear which of the Sama River's tributaries should be regarded as the border. In 1922, Chile and Peru submitted to arbitration by US President Coolidge who determined that none of the tributaries conformed to the Treaty's border description. However, three years later in 1925, he delivered an award that instituted a boundary based on the Sama River to the extent that it conformed to the Treaty description, as well as historical boundary lines of Peruvian provinces as they existed in 1883.[193]

With respect to the southern boundary of the territory covered by Article 3 of the Treaty of Ancón, Chile asked the arbitrator to appoint an expert commission to fix the line. The arbitrator came to the conclusion that it was impossible to fix this line given the data submitted to him. Nevertheless, he ruled that this southern boundary was the same as the historical Peruvian provincial boundary.[194]

190 *The Chamizal Case* (*Mexico/United States*) (1911) XI UNRIAA 309.

191 *Id.*, at 314.

192 Treaty of Peace between Chile and Peru (Treaty of Ancón), 20 October 1883 (Peru, Ministerio de Relaciones Exteriores (1936) *Tratados, convenciones y acuerdosvigentes entre el Perú y otros estados I*, Lima: Imprenta Torres Aguirre: 165–168).

193 *Tacna-Arica Question* (*Chile/Peru*) (1925) II UNRIAA 921.

194 *Id.*, at 957.

Finally, in the operative part of his award, the arbitrator reserved the right to appoint a special three-member commission to draw the boundary lines requested by Chile above, in accordance with the arbitral award. With two party-appointed members, the third would be designated by the arbitrator.[195] Thus, while the previous case incorporated expertise into the tribunal, the arbitrator in this case opted to rely on an expert commission to be appointed by him, if the need arose. This is a mode of expert involvement in implementing rather than resolving a dispute that has found favour in future cases. This process of experts implementing the award or judgment to demarcate a boundary can be seen again years later before the ICJ in *Burkina Faso/Niger* (see Part 3.7 above).

4.3 *Trail Smelter Arbitration (United States of America/Canada)*

Another early but landmark case was the *Trail Smelter* arbitration,[196] dealing with a dispute between the United States and Canada, concerning, among other things, the pollution of the Columbia River by sulphides. In this case, sulphur dioxide fumes emitted by a privately-owned zinc and lead smelter located next to the Columbia River in a place called Trail in Canada, close to the US border, were carried by the prevailing winds across the border into the US state of Washington. These fumes caused damage to privately-owned crops and timber. On assessing the evidence, the arbitral tribunal found no demonstrable harm to the river, though it did find that damage had indeed occurred in the US state of Washington, for which Canada was liable to pay compensation.[197]

The tribunal observed that a balance had to be struck between the interests of industry and the agricultural community.[198] In this regard, it took note of the parties' desire to reach a 'just solution', which it interpreted to mean one that would allow the continuance of the operation of the Trail Smelter, but under such restrictions and limitations as would, as far as foreseeable, prevent damage in the United States, and as would enable indemnity to be obtained, if, in spite of such restrictions and limitations, damage should occur in the future in the United States.[199]

The *Trail Smelter* tribunal made a pertinent observation about the evidence submitted to it. While experts on both sides provided valuable evidence as to the actual condition of crops in the field, these observations were not made continuously in any crop season or in all parts of the area of probable damage.

---

195 *Id.*
196 *Trail Smelter Arbitration (United States v. Canada)* (1941) 3 UNRIAA 1905.
197 *Id.*, at 1931–1932.
198 McCaffrey, *supra* note 27, at 262.
199 *Trail Smelter Arbitration*, *supra* note 196, at 1938–1939.

Moreover, the observations 'were not made simultaneously by the experts for the two countries, who acted separately and without comparing their conclusions with each other contemporaneously'.[200] Furthermore, while the experts testified to a great length about the effects of sulphur dioxide fumigations on trees in the forests, they remained in disagreement as to the cause of the poor condition of the trees – either sulphur dioxide fumes (US experts) or the ravages of insects, diseases, droughts or fires (Canadian experts).[201] In general, the expert witnesses 'expressed contrary views and arrived at opposite conclusions, on most of the questions relating to cause of injury'.[202] The tribunal was of the view that the experts were 'completely honest and sincere in their views and that the expert witnesses arrived at their conclusions as the integral result of their high technical skill'. At the same time, the tribunal relied on a US District Court ruling that said,

> It must not be overlooked that witnesses who give opinion evidence are sometimes unconsciously influenced by their environment, and their evidence colored, if not determined, by their point of view. The weight to be given to such evidence must be determined in the light of the knowledge, the training, the power of observation and analysis, and in general the mental equipment, of each witness, assuming, as I do, that the witnesses of the respective parties were honest and intended to testify to the truth as they perceived it.... The real value I find in the testimony of these opinion witnesses of the parties lies in their description of appearances and statement of the surrounding circumstances, rather than in their ultimate expressed opinions. I have no doubt of the accuracy of the experiments made by the expert and scientific witnesses called by the parties.[203]

The tribunal also appointed two technical consultants to assist it, especially in implementing the decision.[204] The oldest environmental precedent for the use of tribunal-appointed experts,[205] the significance of the tribunal's treatment of the technical evidence is best summed up by Boyle: '[T]he *Trail Smelter* case

200 *Id.*, at 1921.

201 *Id.*: 'It is possible that each side laid somewhat too great emphasis on the causes for which it contended'.

202 *Id.*, at 1922.

203 United States District Court, *Anderson v. American Smelting & Refining Co.*, 265 Federal Reporter 928 (Judge Johnson).

204 *Trail Smelter Arbitration*, *supra* note 196, at 1934–1935.

205 A. Boyle & J. Harrison, *'Judicial Settlement of International Environmental Disputes: Current Problems'*, 4 Journal of International Dispute Settlement (2013) 245–276, at 273.

shows how legal and technical expertise can be blended in an international arbitration to produce an award that is competent and creative in both fields'.[206] This is also a landmark decision with respect to the genesis and development of the 'no harm principle'[207] in the context of transboundary environmental damage.[208]

4.4 *Zarumilla River Case* (*Peru v. Ecuador*)

The Zarumilla River forms a portion of the boundary between Ecuador and Peru. In the mid-twentieth century, the two countries submitted a dispute concerning the river to arbitration by the Chancellery of Brazil. The award was rendered in 1945 and accepted by both parties.

The Protocol of Peace, Friendship, and Boundaries between Peru and Ecuador[209] laid out a description of a boundary line between the two countries. However, it was also understood that the line described by technical experts on the ground would be accepted by Peru and Ecuador for the demarcation of the boundary between the two countries.[210] However, the naval captain who served as sole arbitrator rendered his award apparently without expert assistance.

The approach taken by the arbitrator in this case is a deviation from the decisions that preceded it, all of which rely on expert assistance in one form or another. While both parties accepted this award, it could be argued that expert involvement in demarcation of the boundary may have helped in producing a more legitimate decision. However, it must also be noted that the sole arbitrator was not a lawyer but a naval captain, and his knowledge and experience may have substituted, to some extent, for the necessary expertise in boundary demarcation.

---

206 A. Boyle, 'Environmental Dispute Settlement', *Max Planck Encyclopedia of Public International Law* (Oxford: Oxford University Press, 2009), para. 12.

207 *Trail Smelter Arbitration, supra* note 196, at 1965:

> under the principles of international law ... no state has the right to use or permit the use of its territory in such a manner as to cause injury by fumes in or to the territory of another or the properties or persons therein, when the case is of serious consequence and the injury is established by clear and convincing evidence.

208 For a discussion of this principle and its development, see S. M. A. Salman, '*The Obligation Not to Cause Significant Harm (Article 7)*', in L. Boisson de Chazournes, M. Moïse Mbengue, M. Tignino, K. Sangbana & J. Rudall (eds.), *The UN Convention on the Law of the Non-Navigational Uses of International Watercourses: A Commentary* (Oxford: Oxford University Press, 2019) 95–122, at 96–100.

209 Protocol of Peace, Friendship, and Boundaries between Peru and Ecuador (Rio Protocol) 29 January 1942 ((1942) 36 AJIL 168).

210 *Ruling Concerning the Disagreement between Ecuador and Peru over the Zamora-Santiago Sector* (1945) XXVIII UNRIAA 413, at 418.

4.5 *Lac Lanoux Arbitration* (*Spain v. France*)

In the *Lac Lanoux* arbitration,[211] Spain alleged that France was misusing the River Carol by diverting it and returning it to its original course with a different composition and quality. The tribunal rejected that argument, finding that there was no change to the composition of the water and no pollution had been established.

This dispute centred on a French project for diversion of the waters of Lake Lanoux, which is located in the Pyrenees. A pre-existing treaty between France and Spain regulated certain transboundary issues, including the apportionment of water.[212] In 1950, the French government presented a plan aiming to exploit the hydroelectric potential of Lake Lanoux by diverting its waters towards another river, thereby affecting the course of waters that naturally drained into Spanish territory via the Carol River.[213] Although the French project also ensured the full restoration of flow to the Carol River, it met with opposition from the Spanish government. While France offered to return to the River Carol an amount of water equivalent to that which had been diverted, Spain opposed any diversion of Lake Lanoux waters on the ground that the project would alter the natural conditions of the hydrographic basin of Lake Lanoux by diverting its waters to the other river. Thus, by making restitution of the waters to the River Carol physically dependent upon human will, 'which would result in the de facto preponderance of one party only, rather than in the preservation of the equality of the two parties'.[214] In particular, Spain argued that, under the provisions of the Treaty of Bayonne of 1866,[215] the works affecting transboundary waters could only be executed with its consent. The *ad hoc* arbitral tribunal constituted to resolve this dispute concluded that the French project did not violate the 1866 Treaty.[216] Delegations of the parties included experts who were government employees.

The formulation of the question posed to the tribunal in the *compromis* limited the competence of the tribunal to the application and interpretation of a treaty.[217] Similar to a few cases discussed above, the decision hinged on principles of international law such as riparian rights under international law and good faith and was not predicated on complex facts and thus did not need to rely on experts for its successful resolution.

211 Lake Lanoux Arbitration (Spain/France) (1957) XII UNRIAA 281.

212 Boisson de Chazournes, *supra* note 44, at 210.

213 *Id.*

214 McCaffrey, *supra* note 27, at 255.

215 Treaty on Boundaries between Spain and France from the Valley of Andorra to the Mediterranean (with additional act) (Treaty of Bayonne), 26 May 1866, 1288 *UNTS* 305.

216 *Lake Lanoux Arbitration*, *supra* note 211, at 306–307.

217 McCaffrey, *supra* note 27, at 256.

4.6 *Argentina/Chile Frontier Case*

By a *compromis* of 1965, Argentina and Chile agreed to submit to arbitration the delimitation of certain portions of the frontier line between the two countries.[218] The course of the boundary ran through the rivers Palena, Encuentro, and Engano. This demarcation involved the interpretation of an earlier arbitral award of 1902. The arbitrator, Queen Elizabeth II of the United Kingdom, had to determine the course of the boundary between two boundary posts, which in the first section resulted the thalweg of the Encuentro River and from there the land water-parting between both countries. The Queen delegated her duty as arbitrator to a three-member tribunal that she appointed. Both the Argentine and Chilean delegations included geographers as experts.[219] For a tribunal-ordered field mission and air survey of the disputed area, both parties added geographic and cartographic experts on their delegations.[220] Moreover, the tribunal appointed a number of engineers to its staff by an Order, before embarking on this field mission.[221]

The tribunal's final decision and demarcation of the course of the boundary was rendered ostensibly without any further assistance from experts. It appears, however, that apart from party experts, they had easy recourse to expert advice on their staff. It is interesting to note here that these staff experts were appointed transparently with a tribunal order.

4.7 *Gut Dam Arbitration* (*Canada/United States of America*)

This arbitration between Canada and the United States[222] involved the question of damage caused to property in the United States allegedly as a result of flooding caused by a Canadian dam (the Gut Dam) built across the international boundary in the international section of the St. Lawrence River.[223]

The Lake Ontario Claims Tribunal that the parties established heard claims on behalf of US citizens for flooding and erosion damage to property. The questions before the Tribunal concerned matters such as the class of persons entitled to compensation under the agreement, whether the obligations of Canada were temporally limited, whether the dam had caused the damage complained of, and the amount of compensation that was due.[224]

Canada's arguments were predicated on the proper interpretation of US government documents executed for approving Canadian plans for construction

218 *Argentine-Chile Frontier Case* (1966) XVI UNRIAA 109.
219 *Id.*, at 115.
220 *Id.*, at 147.
221 *Id.*, at 122.
222 *Gut Dam Arbitration* [1968] 4 *ILM* 118 (1969).
223 McCaffrey, *supra* note 27, at 264.
224 *Id.*, at 265–266.

of the dam.[225] An important question of causation arose as to whether water had risen in the Great Lakes region generally in the past few years,[226] and thus whether the flooding could entirely or in part be attributed to the Gut Dam. This is a question of fact which would have determined the question of liability and thereby compensation. Unfortunately, the role of expert advice in such a situation will remain unknown for this specific case, since it was settled after a few interim decisions from the Tribunal.

4.8 *Rhine Chlorides Arbitration*

The *Rhine Chlorides Arbitration* concerned the auditing of accounts between the Netherlands and France pursuant to the Additional Protocol of 1991 to the 1976 Convention on the Protection of the Rhine against Pollution by Chlorides.[227] The issues in this case involved water protection closely intertwined with economic factors.[228] The Convention and its 1991 Protocol aimed to improve water quality by taking measures against pollution by chlorides. The Protocol set out a system of allocation of payments by participating countries in furtherance of this aim. The dispute between the two states in this arbitration arose out of a difference in interpretation and application of the Protocol with respect to modalities of payment.

The tribunal's analysis is entirely related to treaty interpretation and application of principles of international law. Except for the occasional mention of financial experts in relation to calculation of compensation, there is no reference to experts. This could be cited as yet another example of a water dispute based almost entirely on principles of water law or treaty law or international law in general, rather than requiring much fact-finding from the tribunal.

However, chapter VI of the award itself is illustrative of the possible need for experts. The tribunal found that it 'has no means of determining the cost overruns resulting from the rise in prices after 1998, since these depend on the rate at which product is removed from storage and the rate of inflation'.[229] The tribunal left this to the parties to determine. It is hard to imagine that with some expert assistance this figure could not be calculated.

---

225 *Gut Dam Arbitration*, *supra* note 222, at 120.

226 McCaffrey, *supra* note 27, at 267.

227 *Rhine Chlorides Arbitration Concerning the Auditing of Accounts* (*The Netherlands/France*) (11 March 2004) PCA Case No. 2000–02.

228 Boisson de Chazournes, *supra* note 44, at 210.

229 *Rhine Chlorides Arbitration*, *supra* note 227, at 66–67.

4.9 *Abyei Arbitration (Government of Sudan/Sudan People's Liberation Movement/Army)*

This dispute is unique in terms of its parties. While one party is a state (Sudan), the other was a non-state entity, the Sudan People's Liberation Movement/ Army (SPLM). Under the institutional guidance of the PCA, these two entities submitted their dispute regarding boundary demarcation in the Abyei area. A number of waterways and channels in the area under question make this arbitration relevant for the purposes of our discussion.

The first internal boundary dispute submitted to international arbitration, the Abyei area that became the subject matter of this arbitration was in dispute both in terms of its size and its boundaries. Before coming to arbitration, this dispute arose as a result of disagreement over the boundaries between North and South Sudan in the Abyei area between the Sudan government and SPLM while negotiating an end to their civil war. One of the important markers in the Abyei area was the Bahr el Arab River. The Sudan government considered only the area south of this river to be the Abyei area, thus making the river the natural boundary between northern and southern Sudan. The SPLM on the other hand insisted that the area was far larger than that proposed by the Sudan government, which led to a deadlock.[230]

The first attempt at resolving this dispute was the establishment of the Abyei Boundaries Commission (ABC). The ABC consisted of fifteen members, five each appointed by the parties, and five impartial experts appointed by the United States and the United Kingdom. The ABC would be chaired by one of the experts. The 'experts' referred to in this context were knowledgeable in history, geography and other relevant expertise. The ABC was to hear testimony from representatives of the people of Abyei and its neighbours and the two conflicting parties, and to consult relevant sources on Sudan. Its report would be considered final and binding. The two parties agreed on the rules of procedure for the ABC, which contained descriptions of the ABC's work programme, including field visits, hearings of presentations by representatives of both sides, and, finally, evaluation of the evidence and preparation of a final report. The ABC was to endeavour to reach a decision by consensus, but if this was not possible, the experts would have the final say. However, the other 10 members of the ABC would continue to be part of the process of hearings, field visits, and deliberations.

---

230 S. M. A. Salman, *'The Abyei Territorial Dispute between North and South Sudan: Why Has Its Resolution Proven Difficult?'*, in J. Unruh and R. C. Williams (eds.), *Land and Post-Conflict Peacebuilding* (Abingdon: Routledge, 2013) 25–68, at 30.

The report of the ABC, issued in 2005, did not bring about peaceful resolution of the dispute over the Abyei area.[231] It rejected the Sudan government's claim that Abyei was limited to the land south of the Bahr el Arab River. The government thus rejected the report, claiming that the ABC had exceeded its mandate, while the SPLM accepted it as final and binding.

Therefore, to settle this renewed dispute and to quell the fighting that broke out in the Abyei area, the parties agreed, among other things, to submit the dispute over the findings of the ABC to binding arbitration.[232] The PCA is uniquely positioned to administer a dispute of this nature, with its optional rules for arbitrations with only one party as a state.[233]

This case becomes even more important when we examine the extent and use of experts in the proceedings. A wealth of information on written and oral expert proceedings can be found from a close examination of the case documents.

In the *Abyei* arbitration, Sudan appended an expert report by an expert surveyor and geographer to its memorial. The SPLM, the other party in this arbitration, also included an expert report. Both these reports had supplementary reports in replies and rejoinders. These experts (among others) were part of the delegations of the two parties, but also presented for cross-examination by the opposing party.[234] The tribunal also asked the PCA Secretariat about the possibility of assistance from cartographers and geographers for preparation of the award.[235] This would enable the tribunal to operate within the prescribed time limits.[236] The PCA appointed two experts to assist the tribunal and forwarded their curriculum vitae to the parties.[237] Draft terms of reference were also circulated to the parties for comments and outlined the role that the tribunal envisaged for the experts in this dispute.[238]

The procedural order appointing the experts included a declaration from the experts that they would 'perform their duties honorably and faithfully,

231 *Id.*, at 35.

232 *Id.*, at 38–39.

233 PCA Optional Rules for Arbitrating Disputes between Two Parties of Which Only One is a State (1993), available at http://pca-cpa.org/wp-content/uploads/sites/6/2016/01/Optional-Rules-for-Arbitrating-Disputes-between-Two-Parties-of-Which-Only-One-is-a-State-1993.pdf; accessed 17 July 2019.

234 Salman, *supra* note 230, paras. 81–82.

235 See, PCA Optional Rules between Two Parties of Which Only One is a State, *supra* note 233, art. 27.

236 *Abyei Arbitration* (*Sudan v. The Sudan People's Liberation Movement/Army*), Award [2009] ICGJ 422 (PCA), para. 74.

237 *Id.*, para. 75.

238 *Id.*

impartially and conscientiously', as well as a duty of confidentiality.[239] These experts were expected to assist the tribunal in delimiting boundaries on a map, make themselves available to assist the tribunal as required in the preparation of the award, and to 'perform their duties according to best international practices in their fields of expertise'.[240]

The tribunal in this case, too, opted for a passive treatment of scientific evidence, interpreting its mandate as excluding 'an analysis of the substantive correctness' of scientific facts. Thus, it decided not to engage 'in an omnibus reopening of'[241] the appreciation of scientific evidence. Nevertheless, the scientific evidence, which the tribunal found to be scarce[242] and 'marked, in varying degrees, by some imprecision,'[243] was eventually found to be germane to deciding the case.

In the *Abyei* arbitration, in keeping with procedural order no. 1, each party was allotted a maximum of 5 hours and 45 minutes for the oral round involving experts. Cross-examination by each party of the other party's witnesses would be deducted from the former's time. Thirty minutes of time was allotted for questions from the tribunal and other contingencies. To maintain the efficiency of this round of pleading, the tribunal chairman requested that each party be mindful of the time limitations mentioned and manage their presentation and cross-examination times judiciously. The expert made a solemn declaration before commencing his presentation.[244] It did not include a declaration of honesty as in the oral proceedings in most other disputes. He then proceeded to give an introductory speech regarding his background and curriculum vitae before starting the presentation. After he was cross-examined, Sudan ended with a brief re-examination. The tribunal took the opportunity to itself question the expert at the end. A similar procedure was followed for the four other experts, though not all provided detailed background information on themselves.

Thus, it appears that the procedure followed for party experts in this case was broadly similar to that seen at the ICJ, though with peculiarities of its own. The tribunal's own experts were also used in a manner similar to the limited practice seen at the ICJ, though the scope of their work was laid out quite broadly in the terms of reference. These experts were required to help the tribunal in delimiting boundaries on a map and to remain available to assist

239 *Id.*, para. 77.

240 *Id.*

241 *Id.*, paras. 410–411.

242 *Id.*, para. 455.

243 *Id.*, para. 534.

244 'I solemnly declare upon my honour and conscience that my statement will be in accordance with my sincere belief'.

the tribunal in preparing its award. Aside from the scope of the experts' work, which made their tasks clear, it is not explicit from the award the exact manner in which the experts were of assistance to the tribunal.

This tribunal found that the ABC had exceeded its mandate in certain respects. Its award, however, while accepted by the disputing parties, was not universally accepted by all stakeholders. One of the northern tribes deeply involved in the dispute rejected the decision on the ground that the territory delimited by the PCA tribunal award as the Abyei area gave too much of their own land and villages to a southern tribe and restricted their grazing rights. Therefore, even an award accepted by both disputing parties was not implemented, and the boundaries were not demarcated in the Abyei area. The political process to follow, that is a referendum to decide on the part of Sudan to which Abyei would belong, did not take place since the northern tribe in opposition to the PCA award disagreed on who the residents of the Abyei area were. Thus, even after the ABC report and the PCA award, the dispute remained unresolved.

4.10 *Experts in Disputes under the Indus Waters Treaty* (*Pakistan/India*)

A rare treaty provision, yet to gain popularity, is the one in the Indus Waters Treaty of 1960, between India and Pakistan. The unique multi-tier dispute settlement system under the Indus Waters Treaty has already been described in Part 2.3 above.

Before the need for this court of arbitration arises, however, the first port of call in case of a difference of opinion or 'question' under this treaty is the Permanent Indus Commission.[245] If the Commission cannot reach agreement on the question, the next stage is reference to a Neutral Expert. Annexure G of the Treaty, in establishing a court of arbitration for possible disputes arising out of this treaty, envisages the appointment of a 'highly qualified engineer' to the tribunal.[246] This was successfully applied in the *Kishenganga* arbitration,[247] but is not yet a widely-found provision in treaties or other international legal texts. As the expert member of this court of arbitration noted, 'such an expert may facilitate other members' understanding of the issues, undertake technical analysis, assist colleagues in weighing the credibility of scientific evidence and check facts and analysis'.[248] Differences have arisen and been resolved

245 Indus Waters Treaty, *supra* note 22, art. IX(1).

246 Indus Waters Treaty, *supra* note 22, Annexure G, para. 4(b)(ii).

247 *Indus Waters Kishenganga Arbitration* (*Pakistan v. India*), Final Award [2013] ICGJ 478 (PCA).

248 A. Keene, *'Outcome Paper for the Seminar on the International Court of Justice at 70: In Retrospect and in Prospect'*, 7:2 Journal of International Dispute Settlement (2016) 238–265, at 255.

both under the Neutral Expert system (see Part 4.10.1 below) and disputes by the court of arbitration (see Part 4.10.2 below). Each is unique in its own way, and they are discussed below.

4.10.1 Baglihar Neutral Expert Determination

In 2005, following the failure to resolve the issue through the Permanent Indus Commission, Pakistan requested that the World Bank appoint a Neutral Expert on the ground that a difference had arisen with India under Article IX(2) of the Indus Waters Treaty relating to India's Baglihar hydroelectric plant on the River Chenab. In Pakistan's view, the question had risen to the status of a difference that needed resolution by a Neutral Expert. This was the first time that this procedure was invoked under the Treaty.[249] Failing consensus by the parties on the individual to be appointed, and on a third party to appoint the Neutral Expert, the Expert was appointed by the World Bank.

The crux of this difference related to India's planned construction of a dam (the Baglihar Dam) on the River Chenab, one of the western rivers that was allocated to Pakistan under the Indus Waters Treaty. India claimed that it had the right to build upstream storage facilities on this river under the Treaty. Pakistan was concerned that this construction would lead to water shortages for it, downstream.

The World Bank went through a complex process over three months before appointing the Expert. The first stage involved two rounds of claims and counter-claims from the two parties, beginning with Pakistan's request to appoint a Neutral Expert. Thereafter, the Bank indicated that all communications related to this proceeding would be trilateral, shared among both parties and the Bank. Pakistan, meanwhile, sought an interim order from the Bank to ask India to halt constructions on the Baglihar Dam until the Neutral Expert's decision. Unfortunately, as the Bank noted, this was outside its powers, and was confined to the Neutral Expert's role. Thereafter, studying all documents submitted by the parties and seeking a second opinion from an ICJ judge, the Bank concluded that it was required to appoint a Neutral Expert under the Treaty. The next step in the process involved creating a shortlist of engineers, interviewing them for conflicts of interest, and ensuring their availability to serve as Neutral Expert. To fulfil the requirement of 'consultation' with the parties under the treaty, the Bank decided to submit three names at a time from this shortlist, to the parties for them to agree on a candidate.[250] The parties agreed on a name from the very first list – Professor Raymond Lafitte of the Federal Institute of Technology, Lausanne.

---

249 McCaffrey, *supra* note 27, at 268.

250 Salman & Uprety, *'Shared Watercourses'*, *supra* note 23, at 29–30.

Professor Lafitte was informed that he would not receive technical or legal advice from the World Bank, and he was advised to obtain the consent of the parties before appointing an assistant and a legal advisor, if he so wished. This lengthy process of appointment of the Neutral Expert has been said to demonstrate how his role has transformed from a simple administrative role as conceived under the Treaty to a quasi-judicial task in practice.[251]

The Neutral Expert was required to deal with six issues in the Expert Determination, which was published within two years of appointment. One of the most important issues was related to the method of sediment control designed by India for the Baglihar Dam. Given the large amount of sediment carried by Himalayan rivers, India had designed the dam with low outlets that would make possible drawdown sluicing or flushing, techniques that pass accumulated sediment through the dam during periods of high flow, mainly in the monsoon season. Pakistan alleged that this, and other aspects of the Dam's design were not permitted by the Indus Treaty. Pakistan made clear during the negotiation of the 1960 Treaty that it was crucial for it that the projects India would be allowed to construct on the western rivers (such as the Chenab) should not result in a decreased flow to Pakistan or change significantly its timing.[252] This resulted in requirements that limited 'live' storage behind India's dams, that is, storage that is capable of manipulation, and the restriction of the types of dams India could construct on these rivers to those dams that do not store water but rather pass it through turbines to produce electricity. The Treaty generally only permits water storage that is not for operational purposes.[253] This effectively functions as a floor on top of which the flow used to operate the run-of-the-river plant passes. Drawdown sluicing or flushing would lower this floor to as much as the bottom of the reservoir during the flushing operation. This would increase the volume of water reaching Pakistan downstream significantly during the sluicing or flushing operation, a cause of concern for Pakistan.[254]

Keeping in mind the quick resolution of the difference envisaged in the Treaty, the Expert met the parties to decide the basic rules and procedures for the conduct of the process. Subsequent to receiving parties' submissions, he visited the Baglihar site together with the parties. A few more meetings led to the Expert submitting his draft determination to the parties, a process only

251 *Id.*, at 30; S. M. A. Salman, *'The Baglihar Difference and Its Resolution Process – A Triumph for the Indus Waters Treaty?'*, 10:2 Water Policy (2008) 105–117, at 110.

252 McCaffrey, *supra* note 27, at 268.

253 Indus Waters Treaty, *supra* note 22, Annexure D, para. 2(a).

254 McCaffrey, *supra* note 27, at 269.

seen in the World Trade Organization dispute settlement process (interim report). Subsequent to the parties' comments, the Expert finalized his report.[255]

Despite his background and profession as an engineer, the Neutral Expert's Determination was not only fact-based. Undoubtedly under the guidance of his appointed legal advisor, he relied on the Vienna Convention on the Law of Treaties as customary international law and carried out treaty interpretation as well.[256] He determined that the rights and obligations of Pakistan and India 'should be read in the light of new technical norms and new standards as provided for by the Treaty'.[257] This led him to the conclusion that '[t]he rights and obligations contained in Part 3 of Annexure D must be interpreted so as to allow for the fulfilling of the object(s) and purpose(s) of the Treaty …, taking into account the best and latest practices in the field of construction and operation of hydro-electric plants'.[258]

Among the various findings that led to his conclusions, the Expert noted the change in reservoir sedimentation management over the past 20 years, and that the Treaty reflected the status of technology on this matter from the 1950s.[259] In the Expert's opinion, 'sound operation of the outlets will necessitate carrying out maintenance of the reservoir with drawdown sluicing each year during the monsoon season. The reservoir level should be drawn down to a level of … 17 m below that of the Dead Storage Level'. This sediment control technique is not permitted by the Treaty, according to the court of arbitration that heard the Kishenganga dispute. However, this decision is final and binding upon the parties and upon any court of arbitration established under the Indus Waters Treaty.[260]

Notwithstanding the weight of the final outcome of this Expert Determination, in inter-state disputes this is a rarely used means of settling disputes and may prove to be an efficient and quick means of settling differences in water-related or similar scientific disputes.

---

255 Salman, *'The Baglihar Difference'*, *supra* note 251, at 112–113.

256 R. Lafitte, Baglihar Hydroelectric Plant, Expert Determination on points of difference referred by the Government of Pakistan under the provisions of the Indus Waters Treaty, Executive Summary, Lausanne, 12 February 2007, available at http://siteresources.worldbank.org/SOUTHASIAEXT/Resources/223546-1171996340255/BaglIharSummary.pdf.

257 *Id.*, at 5.

258 *Id.*

259 *Id.*, at 12.

260 Indus Waters Treaty, *supra* note 22, Annexure F, para. 11.

4.10.2 Kishenganga Arbitration

The *Indus Waters Kishenganga* arbitration was unique in the sense of expertise being built into the tribunal (the 'court of arbitration') by virtue of the special provisions in the Indus Waters Treaty.[261] This court of arbitration is to be composed of seven members, with two arbitrators appointed by each party, and three 'umpires', one of whom would be well-versed in international law, another a highly qualified engineer, and the third qualified by status and reputation to be chair of the court of arbitration who may, but need not, be an engineer or lawyer.[262] These three umpires were selected through the procedures and by the appointing authorities specified in paragraph 7 of Annexure G of the Treaty.

The Kishenganga dispute arose out of Pakistan's claims concerning India's hydroelectric project activities in the Kashmir region, similar to the Baglihar Dam case. Specifically, the claim related to whether India's planned diversion of the River Kishenganga breached its treaty obligations (such as maintenance of natural channels and non-interference with rivers in the region).[263]

The court of arbitration found that India was required to preserve downstream flows for two purposes: to protect Pakistan's rights under the Treaty;[264] and to protect the environment as required by customary international law.[265] The tribunal did not confine itself to requesting data related to environmental concerns, but also wanted to know more about the effect of various levels of minimum flows on power generation at both the Indian and Pakistani hydroelectric projects and agricultural uses by Pakistan. Unique not only for an arbitral tribunal but for international courts in general,[266] this court of arbitration also set up a review mechanism, permitting, seven years after diversion of the Kishenganga through the hydroelectric project, reconsideration of its determination of minimum flow of water through the Permanent Indus Commission and subsequent procedures set out in the Indus Treaty.[267] Indeed, from an environmental point view, the recognition of the principle of the minimum

261 *Id.*, Annexure G, para. 4.
262 *Id.*
263 Boisson de Chazournes, *supra* note 44, at 212.
264 See especially Partial Award, *Indus Waters Kishenganga Arbitration* (*Pakistan v. India*), Record of Proceedings (2010–2013), PCA Award Series, Case No. 2011–01 (2014), paras. 281–282.
265 *Id.*, paras. 290–293.
266 McCaffrey, *supra* note 27, at 281.
267 *Indus Waters Kishenganga Arbitration* Record of Proceedings (2010–2013), *supra* note 264, para. 459; *Indus Waters Kishenganga Arbitration*, Final Award, *supra* note 247, para. 461.

environmental flow in a river is the most significant aspect of the award rendered by this court of arbitration.[268]

Among the members of the court of arbitration, one of the three appointed 'umpires' was required to be a highly qualified engineer.[269] The chair of the court was required to be a person qualified by status and reputation to be chair of the court of arbitration who may, but need not, be an engineer or lawyer.[270] In this dispute, he was not. Nevertheless, one of the seven-member court was a 'highly qualified engineer', appointed by the procedure laid down in the Treaty.[271] Both parties also included technical experts/advisers on their delegations and also presented expert witnesses.[272] A site visit was also conducted, where all the members of the court were present. This technique of using expertise built into the tribunal has been considered a more useful form of using expert assistance than tribunal-appointed experts, in case of non-appearance of a party, as in the *South China Sea* arbitration.[273] Indeed, the non-legal adjudicator played an important role in enhancing the tribunal's competence in scientific fact-finding,[274] which received great praise in scholarly writing.[275] The method of work of this court of arbitration was also commended for the transparency it achieved by properly documenting how the expert adjudicator evaluated and assessed certain technical issues in the partial award and the final award.[276]

This dispute also saw the oft-repeated argument (by India in this case) regarding the tribunal's competence to adjudicate on an issue involving highly technical aspects. The court of arbitration ruled that the

> very composition of a court of arbitration also points to its competence in technical matters. In general, the skills or qualifications required of

268 M. Tignino, *'Le fleuve Indus et ses usages: L'arbitrage relatif aux eaux du fleuve Kishenganga'*, 60 Annuaire français de droit international (2014) 519–542.

269 Indus Waters Treaty, *supra* note 22, Annexure G, para. 4(b)(ii).

270 *Id.*, Annexure G, para. 4(b)(i).

271 *Id.*, Annexure G, para. 7.

272 *Indus Waters Kishenganga Arbitration*, Partial Award, *supra* note 264.

273 X. Ma, *'Introducing Non-Legal Adjudicators as a Counterbalanced Measure for Non-Appearance in Inter-State Adjudication and Arbitration'*, 14:2 Transnational Dispute Management (2016) 1–23, at 16.

274 *Id.*, at 18.

275 K. Fach Gómez, *'The US-EU Transatlantic Trade and Investment Partnership: Should It Leave a Door Open for Non-Legal Arbitrators?'*, 34:2 Conflict Resolution Quarterly (2016) 189–223; *J. R. Crook, 'In Re Indus Waters Kishenganga Arbitration (Pakistan v. India)'*, 108:2 American Journal of International Law (2014) 308–314, at 314; B. Sidhu, *'The Kishenganga Arbitration: Transboundary Water Resources Governance'*, 43:3 Environmental Policy and Law (2013) 147–161, at 153.

276 Ma, *supra* note 273, at 19.

> the members of a commission or tribunal represent a probative indication of the role the Parties intended that body to perform. Here, one of the Court's umpires is required to be a 'highly qualified engineer,' and, indeed, nothing would stop the Parties from appointing engineers as their Party-appointed arbitrators or as the Chairman of the Court … Accordingly, the Court considers that no dispute brought before a court of arbitration could be rendered inadmissible merely on the grounds that it involved a technical question.[277]

Thus, the court of arbitration ruled that not only was the claim admissible, but that it could decide the issue with the support of experts,[278] thereby bringing technical questions squarely within the scope of a judicial tribunal.[279]

An interesting deviation from the general trend above can be seen in case of appointment of the expert arbitrator in the *Indus Waters* arbitration. The criteria for selecting the expert arbitrator were left to the discretion and wisdom of the appointing authority, the Rector of the Imperial College of Science and Technology, London.[280] Interestingly, a potential arbitrator who was a national of either of the two parties could be considered for disqualification only if the person had been employed or retained by either of the parties.[281] The parties could also waive any of the disqualifications of the appointee.[282]

In the *Indus Waters* arbitration both parties included expert reports in their written submissions to the court of arbitration. India objected to Pakistan's notification of a new expert it intended to call at a late stage of the proceedings after the deadline for notification regarding expert witnesses to be called had passed.[283] The court of arbitration decided against permitting this expert to testify, stating that 'permitting such testimony would raise serious issues of procedural fairness'.[284] This was done so that neither party would be surprised by the issues raised, and both parties would have time to adequately prepare. While disallowing this expert's testimony, the court of arbitration left it open to Pakistan to seek to submit a further expert report by this expert if it believed that there were critical matters to the expert's testimony that could not be adequately dealt with through counsel argument during the hearing.

277 *Indus Waters Kishenganga Arbitration*, Partial Award, *supra* note 264, paras. 486–487.
278 *Id.*, para. 487.
279 S. Lorenzmeier, '*Indus Water Kishenganga Arbitration* (*Pakistan v. India*)', *Max Planck Encyclopedia of Public International Law* (Oxford: Oxford University Press, 2015), para. 12.
280 Indus Waters Treaty, *supra* note 22, Appendix to Annexure G.
281 *Id.*, Annexure G, para. 7(b)(iii).
282 *Id.*
283 *Indus Waters Kishenganga Arbitration*, Partial Award, *supra* note 264, paras. 113–114.
284 *Id.*, para. 117.

In this arbitration, by Procedural Order No. 3, the court of arbitration ordered a site visit, which was attended by all the members of the tribunal, and parties' experts, among others. Pursuant to paragraph 3.2 of Procedural Order No. 9, parties conveyed to each other and to the court the names of experts they intended to cross-examine at the hearing on the merits.[285] When Pakistan proposed that India cross-examine a witness via video conference, India argued this would be less effective than in-person examination and would result in prejudicing India. However, by Procedural Order No. 10, the court was of the view that under certain circumstances video conferencing was an acceptable substitute for in-person cross-examination.

> By providing a synchronous audio and visual connection between the witness or expert, the cross-examining counsel, and the arbitral tribunal, video-conferencing can potentially approximate the conditions of in-person cross-examination. The Court notes in this regard that cross-examination of expert and fact witnesses by video-conferencing has been allowed in a number of international arbitral hearings.[286] That said, based on the actual conduct of cross-examination by video-conferencing, the weight to be given to testimony made through that medium rests with the Court.[287]

As mentioned before, this case is landmark from many perspectives. As described above, solely from the perspective of non-legal expertise, both on the bench and in the courtroom, there is much to be learnt from the frameworks and processes used in this dispute.

Further differences have arisen between the two countries on matters related to the Kishenganga Dam and within the scope of the Indus Treaty. They requested the World Bank's assistance in deciding several issues related to this

285 *Id.*, para. 105.

286 ICSID, *Murphy Exploration and Production Company International v. Republic of Ecuador*, ICSID Case No. ARB/08/4 (15 December 2010), para. 16; *Sergei Paushok, CJSC Golden East Company and CJSC Vostokneftegaz Company v. The Government of Mongolia* (28 April 2011) UNCITRAL, available at http://www.italaw.com/sites/default/files/case-documents/ita0622.pdf, accessed 31 January 2019, para. 61; ICSID, *Fraport AG Frankfurt Airport Services Worldwide v. The Republic of the Philippines* ICSID Case No. ARB/03/25 (16 August 2007), para. 43; ICSID, *EDF (Services) Limited v. Romania*, ICSID Case No. ARB/05/13 (8 October 2009), para. 38; ICSID, *SGS Société Générale de Surveillance S A v. The Republic of Paraguay*, ICSID Case No. ARB/07/29 (10 February 2012), para. 23.

287 Article 13(1) of the Supplemental Rules provides that '[t]he Court shall determine the admissibility, relevance, materiality, and weight of the evidence adduced': Supplemental Rules of Procedure, *Indus Waters Kishenganga Arbitration*, Procedural Order No. 2, para. 1.1.

dam, as well as another, the Ratle Hydropower Project, under construction on the Chenab River.[288] The divergences between the parties extend to the mode of dispute settlement. While Pakistan requested a court of arbitration, India sought the appointment of a Neutral Expert by the World Bank. Parallel processes would clearly be unworkable, possibly leading to conflicting decisions, apart from a waste of time and resources. The World Bank's solution was to appoint a third party to assist the two parties to mediate the issues in dispute.[289] It remains to be seen how these existing differences and disputes get resolved, and the role of experts in those processes.

Part 5: Experts in Investor-State Water Disputes

Though not as common, issues relating to water pollution or water access also arise in the investor-state context. A few important cases of this nature, some under the North American Free Trade Agreement (NAFTA) and some under bilateral investment treaties (BITS) are discussed here. Many were conducted under the aegis of ICSID, though some proceeded before the PCA under UNCITRAL Arbitration Rules as well. Before delving into examining the cases, a brief overview of the relevant procedural rules on experts is provided here.

The ICSID Arbitration Rules[290] and ICSID Arbitration (Additional Facility) Rules[291] provide the option for party-appointed and tribunal-appointed experts, though it may be said that the possibility of the tribunal appointing experts is foreseen only because it is not expressly prohibited by the rules, rather than any affirmative statement. NAFTA permits a tribunal to appoint experts for certain kinds of disputes at the request of a disputing party, or *unless a disputing party disapproves*, subject to terms agreed to by the parties.[292]

Provisions in the ICSID Arbitration Rules (as well as the Additional Facility Rules)[293] bear a strong resemblance to key provisions of the ICJ rules governing written and oral proceedings involving experts. Article 32 of the Rules provides for a tribunal to hear experts at oral proceedings.[294] Parties may examine experts under the control of the tribunal president, with any member of the

288 Salman & Uprety *'Shared Watercourses'*, *supra* note 23, at 41.

289 *Id.*, at 43.

290 ICSID Rules of Procedure for Arbitration Proceedings 2006 (ICSID/15 (2006)), arts. 32–36.

291 ICSID Arbitration (Additional Facility) Rules 2006 (ICSID/11 (2006)), arts. 39, 41–43.

292 North American Free Trade Agreement, 17 December 1992, entered into force 1 January 1994, 32 *ILM* 289, 605 (1993), art. 1133.

293 ICSID Arbitration (Additional Facility) Rules, *supra* note 291.

294 ICSID Arbitration Rules, *supra* note 290, art. 32(1); ICSID Arbitration (Additional Facility) Rules, *id.*, art. 39(1).

tribunal being able to question them.[295] Notwithstanding this, a tribunal may admit evidence given by an expert in a written deposition[296] and, with the consent of both parties, may arrange for the examination of an expert otherwise than before the tribunal itself.[297] In the latter situation, the tribunal will define the procedure to be followed and other particulars, and the parties may participate in this examination.[298] This procedure is in the process of being amended to reflect actual practice, with all testimony to be provided in writing, and oral examination of experts as an exception, at the option of the opposing party.[299]

Interestingly, the declaration required of an expert in the ICSID Arbitration Rules[300] excludes the requirement of honesty[301] that is present in the declaration required from a witness, and required from experts at the ICJ. This ICSID rule is more in line with the older ICJ rules which did not consider it important to obtain a declaration of honesty from an expert testifying in court. It is in its scope quite narrow, and is an attempt to assert the expert's independence and neutrality, without explicitly stating so. Criticisms levelled at this declaration may equally apply to this requirement as used by other international fora. An expert's 'sincere belief', while independent of his or her economic relationship with a party, and their testimony impartial in the sense of not being subjectively biased in favour of the appointing party, the declaration remains lacking with respect to the credibility of the expert or the qualification and subsequent admissibility of their statements. Thus, the quality of the expert's testimony, which should be the fundamental basis of the credibility of testimony, remains untested.[302]

In the cases examined in this Part, some were conducted under UNCITRAL Rules, described in Part 4 above, and others under the ICSID Arbitration Rules or ICSID Additional Facility Rules. Part 5.5 below takes a brief look at a few

295 ICSID Arbitration Rules, *id.*, art. 35(1); ICSID Arbitration (Additional Facility) Rules, *id.*, art. 42.

296 ICSID Arbitration Rules, *id.*, art. 36(a); ICSID Arbitration (Additional Facility) Rules, *id.*, art. 43(a).

297 ICSID Arbitration Rules, *id.*, art. 36(b); ICSID Arbitration (Additional Facility) Rules, *id.*, art. 43(b).

298 *Id.*

299 Proposals for Amendment of the ICSID Rules, Working Paper No. 2, Vol. 1 (March 2019), Rule 37.

300 The ICSID Additional Facility Rules make no mention of a declaration for either witness or expert.

301 ICSID Arbitration Rules, *supra* note 290, art. 35(3): 'I solemnly declare upon my honour and conscience that my statement will be in accordance with my sincere belief'.

302 M. Hodgson & M. Stewart, *'Experts in Investor-State Arbitration: The Tribunal as Gatekeeper'*, 9:3 Journal of International Dispute Settlement (2018) 453–463, at 458.

cases related to water law, where experts were not involved, with the goal of examining such situations where experts are not needed, or where they could have been usefully involved.

5.1 *Methanex v. United States of America*

Methanex v. USA is a NAFTA dispute conducted by UNCITRAL Rules. In this dispute, Methanex Corporation, a Canadian company marketing and distributor of methanol (a key component of MTBE, methyl tert-butyl ether) submitted a claim for arbitration for alleged injuries resulting from a Californian ban on the use or sale in California of the gasoline additive MTBE. In particular, when gasoline containing MTBE is discharged into the environment, some of the MTBE may dissolve in the surrounding groundwater, rendering the groundwater unfit for human consumption. In 1999, because of these environmental concerns, California called for the removal of MTBE from gasoline. Following this order, Methanex initiated an arbitration proceeding against the United States.

The tribunal finally rejected all of the investor's claims against the United States. It found that California's actions were not in breach of fair and equitable treatment, since they were within environmental regulatory norms that Methanex should have expected in the absence of any special representations from the United States.[303] Similarly, in its rejection of the investor's expropriation claim, the tribunal gave primacy to California's environmental regulatory authority by (p. 225) finding that the state's concern over MTBE's effect on drinking water justified its regulation with a 'public purpose'.[304]

In *Methanex v. USA*, Methanex submitted nine expert opinions[305] and reports addressing scientific issues surrounding the health and environmental impacts of the gasoline additive MTBE and ethanol. The United States submitted five expert reports, most in rebuttal to Methanex's expert reports.[306] In rejecting the argument that Article 1133 of NAFTA, which provides that the tribunal may appoint an expert witness, limits the tribunal's authority of expert appointment,[307] the tribunal noted that an expert witness appointed by the tribunal is unlike *amicus curiae*. In making that distinction, it noted that an *amicus* might comment on specialized factual matters; however, an *amicus*' role may also be broader than that because an amicus may comment on legal

303 *Methanex Corporation v. United States of America*, Final Award on Jurisdiction and Merits (2005) 44 *ILM* 1345, (UNCITRAL) Part IV, Chapter D, para. 9.

304 *Id.*, para. 7.

305 *Id.*, para. 43.

306 *Id.*, para. 71.

307 Pursuant to the express terms of Article 1133 NAFTA, *supra* note 292, the tribunal cannot appoint experts without the consent of the disputing parties.

issues and may bring a distinct approach to several issues.[308] Another important distinction is that *amici* are advocates and not 'independent' in the sense that they advance a particular case to a tribunal.[309] This set an important precedent with respect to the scope of *amicus* participation in international investment arbitration[310] in particular, but arguably in international dispute settlement generally.

The parties tendered a series of expert reports on scientific issues. In most cases, reply expert reports were also filed by the parties. In these reports, as requested by the tribunal, the experts commented on each other's analyses and opinions. The resulting expert testimony contained in these many reports was extremely important in this arbitration, going to the heart of the question of whether the US measures, as alleged by Methanex, constitute a 'sham environmental protection in order to cater to local political interests or in order to protect a domestic industry'.[311] The way in which this tribunal effectively evaluated the voluminous scientific evidence submitted to it, 'confirmed that the ability of international judicial organs to act as weighers of facts is not a myth nor illusory'.[312]

For example, after reviewing a 600-page report by the University of California (the UC Report), the tribunal considered that it reflected 'a serious, objective and scientific approach to a complex problem in California'. Assessing the way in which this report was subjected to public hearings, testimony and peer review, the tribunal considered that only a serious scientific work could emerge from such an open and informed debate. The oral testimony and cross-examination of expert witnesses on this point also convinced the tribunal of the veracity of this report.[313]

In *Methanex v. USA*, the tribunal set out certain requirements for any expert report that a party may wish to submit. This included an acknowledgment by the expert witness of his or her independent duty to assist the tribunal, overriding any obligation to Methanex as the person engaging or paying that expert witness, and a statement by the expert witness of the truth of his or her opinions and conclusions.[314]

---

308 *Methanex Corporation v. United States of America*, Decision of the Tribunal on Petitions from Third Persons to Intervene as 'Amici Curiae' (UNCITRAL), paras. 36, 38.

309 *Id.*, para. 38.

310 Boisson de Chazournes, *supra* note 44, at 225.

311 *Methanex v. USA*, Final Award, *supra* note 303, para. 41.

312 M. M. Mbengue, *'International Courts and Tribunals as Fact-Finders: The Case of Scientific Fact-Finding in International Adjudication'*, 34:1 Loyola of Los Angeles International and Comparative Law Review (2011) 53–80, at 78.

313 *Methanex v. USA*, Final Award, *supra* note 303, para. 101.

314 *Methanex Corporation v. United States of America*, Partial Award (Preliminary Award on Jurisdiction and Admissibility) (UNCITRAL), para. 165.

By virtue of written agreement between the parties in *Methanex v. USA*, in a joint letter to the tribunal, subject to certain qualifications, Articles 3, 4 and 5 of the International Bar Association's (IBA) Rules on the Taking of Evidence in International Arbitration[315] governed the exchange of documents and presentation of testimony by expert witnesses.[316] In the partial award on jurisdiction and admissibility, the tribunal laid out the requirements for the fresh pleadings to be submitted by Methanex. Depending on the differences between the expert reports adduced by the parties, the tribunal left open the option to make one or more orders under Article 5(3) of the IBA Rules, requesting the expert witnesses to 'meet and confer' and make a joint or supplementary report prior to the main hearing. It asked for submission of all expert witness reports of any person intended by Methanex to provide testimony at an oral hearing on the merits.[317] The expert report was required to be in writing, signed and dated by that expert setting out (i) the full name and address of the expert, present and past relationship with Methanex (if any), and a description of the expert's background, qualifications, training and relevant experience; (ii) a statement of the facts on which the expert witness based his or her expert opinions and conclusions, including (if relevant) a description of the method, materials and other information used in arriving at those opinions and conclusions; (iii) a statement of those expert opinions and conclusions; (iv) an acknowledgment by the expert witness of his or her independent duty to assist the tribunal, including attendance at an oral hearing unless otherwise ordered by the tribunal; and that this duty overrode any obligation to Methanex as the person engaging or paying that expert witness; and (v) a statement by the expert witness of the truth of those opinions and conclusions.[318]

Subsequently, the tribunal ruled that each party's expert reports were required to comply with Article 5 of the IBA Rules. In particular, each expert report was required, by Article 5(2)(b) and (c) of the IBA Rules, to contain a statement of the facts on which it was based, and a description of the evidence and information used in arriving at that report's conclusions. Each party was also required to furnish the tribunal and the opposing party with the scientific papers and reports on which their expert reports were based.

The United States requested an order requiring Methanex to supply all the materials that its scientific experts had relied upon in preparing their expert reports. The United States relied upon paragraph 163 of the Partial Award,

315 International Bar Association (IBA) Rules on the Taking of Evidence in International Arbitration 2010, available at http://www.ibanet.org/Document/Default.aspx?DocumentUid=68336C49-4106-46BF-A1C6-A8F0880444DC; accessed 20 June 2019.

316 *Methanex v. USA*, Final Award, *supra* note 303, para. 10.

317 *Methanex v. USA*, Partial Award, *supra* note 314, para. 163.

318 *Id.*, para. 165.

which required Methanex to file with its fresh pleading 'copies of all evidential documents on which it relies', and Article 3.1 of the IBA Rules. In addition, the United States made a specific request for the underlying programming and key assumptions used in one of the tables to the report of Methanex's expert witness, Professor Rausser.[319] Methanex objected to the United States' request on the basis that it was relying on the expert reports, not on the underlying materials that the expert in question relied on when drafting his or her report. It maintained that, under the IBA Rules,[320] the right of a party to examine information relied on by an expert related only to a tribunal-appointed expert (as opposed to a party-appointed expert witness), and that nothing in the Partial Award or the IBA Rules provided for what was in effect a traditional request for expert discovery by the United States.[321] Methanex also confirmed that all of the material referenced in its expert reports was either publicly available or had been supplied to the United States, save for one specified water control survey of March 2001. The United States responded, arguing *inter alia* that Methanex was plainly relying on the data that its scientists relied upon and that the United States was entitled to know that part of the case that it (the United States) had to meet at the main hearing.[322] The tribunal ordered that Methanex's expert reports (just as with the expert reports of the United States) must comply fully with the requirements of the relevant IBA Rules and the tribunal's orders. With respect to publicly available information, Methanex was ordered to provide identification of this information to the United States and its designated experts. With respect to the water control survey, Methanex was ordered to provide access to this documentation for the United States and its designated experts. No order was made in respect of the table to Professor Rausser's expert report.[323]

For the oral rounds in *Methanex v. USA*, the tribunal divided the time equally between Methanex and United States, subject to the overriding requirement of fairness and recognizing that Methanex would require more time than the United States in cross-examining the designated oral witnesses. It ordered the following examination of expert witnesses: (a) brief examination-in-chief (direct examination) by the United States, (b) cross-examination by Methanex, and (c) re-examination (re-direct) by the United States. While the United States could conduct direct examination, it was nevertheless understood that the existing written statement should stand as evidence-in-chief and that such

319 *Methanex v. USA*, Final Award, *supra* note 303, para. 19.

320 IBA Rules, *supra* note 315, art. 6.5.

321 Article 6.5 of the IBA Rules was not part of the parties' agreement to apply Articles 3, 4 & 5 of the IBA Rules to these proceedings.

322 *Methanex v. USA*, Final Award, *supra* note 303, para. 20.

323 *Id.*, para. 21.

examination-in-chief should therefore not last more than ten minutes without prior permission of the tribunal. It was also understood that the scope of cross-examination should be confined to the scope of the written testimony and any additional evidence-in-chief. Likewise, it was also understood that the scope of any re-examination should be confined to the scope of the cross-examination. Any departure from these understandings would require prior permission of the tribunal and would only be exceptionally granted. Expert witnesses would not be allowed in the hearing room while another expert was being examined, unless the expert in question had already completed his or her testimony. Methanex's experts did not testify orally at the main hearing because the United States did not require their attendance for cross-examination.[324] Thus an expert was only brought in for the various stages of oral proceedings if the opposing party wished to cross-examine the expert. An expert would not be presented in the oral hearings solely for the purpose of examination-in-chief.

A significant departure from other cases was the solemn declaration by an expert in the oral rounds. An expert (referred to as a witness) was brought to the oral proceedings to be examined and cross-examined. The only declaration he made was to speak the truth, and no declaration of 'sincere belief' as is commonly seen for experts in other cases. The following two days, the experts (also referred to as witness) made the solemn declaration of testifying in accordance with their sincere belief. However, there was no declaration to speak the truth.

In *Methanex v. USA*, the United States challenged some of Methanex's expert reports, urging the tribunal to ascribe little weight to them.[325] First, the United States pointed out errors in the reports, then it pointed out certain non-disclosures by the experts, that could affect their independence. Despite the tribunal's clear directive that each expert must disclose their present and past relationship with Methanex,[326] Dr. Pamela Williams' reports did not disclose the fact that her firm had been retained by Methanex since at least 1999 or that Dennis Paustenbach, vice president of a company while Dr. Williams worked there and founder of Dr. Williams' current employer ChemRisk, had been retained by Methanex since at least that date to provide litigation support, apparently for the present case. Dr. Williams' reports also did not disclose

324 *Indus Waters Kishenganga Arbitration*, Final Award, *supra* note 247, para. 42.

325 *Methanex Corporation v. United States of America*, Rejoinder of USA, para. 96.

326 *Methanex v. USA*, Partial Award, *supra* note 314, para. 164(i), 165(i). See also IBA Rules, *supra* note 315, art. 5.2(a); V. V. Veeder, '*Methanex Corporation v. United States of America*, Letter from Tribunal (on Documents Relied upon by Methanex Experts)' (10 October 2003), at 2 (stating that the Tribunal 'expects Methanex's full compliance [with requirements of First Partial Award and IBA Rules for expert witnesses]; and where it has not complied, the Tribunal expects notification of prompt compliance').

that much of the research she relied upon was authored or co-authored by Dr. Paustenbach while on retainer by Methanex.[327]

On the question of admissibility, the United States also submitted a motion to exclude certain of Methanex's evidence. It argued that several expert reports submitted by Methanex failed to comply with the tribunal's directives set forth in the First Partial Award, and the requirements of Articles 4 and 5 of the IBA Rules to which Methanex agreed to adhere. The United States argued that works authored by Dr. Williams should be found inadmissible. Two expert reports were in her own name, and she co-authored four. Each of these reports, according to the United States, failed to comply with the tribunal's requirements in various respects. First, she failed to disclose her present and past relationship with Methanex. Further, one of her reports did not contain an affirmation of truth, and it was not signed. She also failed to confirm her independent duty to the tribunal that overrode any obligation that she had to Methanex. Another expert, Dr. Rausser, failed to conform to these procedural requirements.

Methanex defended its experts in the following manner. Dr. Rausser's reply expert report was deficient in the respects that the United States mentioned. He believed that since these elements were already present in the first expert report, it was not necessary to repeat them in the reply report. Methanex noted that the tribunal did not state that experts were required to repeat these affirmations in their reply reports. Dr. Rausser could submit a supplemental declaration including those statements. The same was the case with Dr. Williams' declarations. With respect to disclosures by Dr. Williams, Methanex contended that she had fully disclosed the relationships that the United States mentioned. According to Methanex, she was not required to make these disclosures in the expert report. The Tribunal did not require that an expert disclose the names of every one of the expert's colleagues and the colleagues' relationships to each of the parties. Thus, Dr. Williams was not required to disclose the relationship between her firm and Methanex. However, she did disclose these relationships in her first report.

The tribunal decided that these two reports under discussion would remain in evidence, 'subject to relevance, materiality and weight'. This indicates that the alleged or possible deficiencies in these reports – relating to independence and disclosure requirements – did not affect the admissibility of the expert reports in question. Further, it is evident from a reading of the final award that the tribunal considered in some detail the opinions put forth in these reports.[328] Indeed, the eventual acceptance or rejection of the various expert

327 *Methanex Corporation v. USA*, Rejoinder of USA, *supra* note 325, para. 97.

328 *Methanex v. USA*, Final Award, *supra* note 303, paras. 59–63, 67–70.

opinions before the tribunal was through a careful weighing and assessment of contradictory opinions, rebuttals and rejoinders.[329]

In its final award, the tribunal very coherently provided its understanding of the scientific evidence submitted to it, along with the oral testimony it heard from the expert witnesses. Having considered all the expert evidence adduced in these proceedings by both parties, the tribunal accepted the UC Report as reflecting a serious, objective and scientific approach. While it accepted the possibility for other scientists and researchers to disagree in good faith with certain of its methodologies, analyses and conclusions, the fact of such disagreement, even if correct, did not warrant the tribunal in treating the UC Report as part of a political sham by California, as alleged by Methanex. In particular, the UC Report was subjected at the time to public hearings, testimony and peer review; its emergence as a serious scientific work from such an open and informed debate was the best evidence that it was not the product of a political sham engineered by California, leading subsequently to the two measures impugned by Methanex in these arbitration proceedings. Moreover, in all material respects, the tribunal was not persuaded that the UC Report was scientifically incorrect. This was due to the scientific expert witnesses presented by the United States and tested under cross-examination by Methanex. The tribunal accepted these experts' conclusions without reservation.[330] Prior to this pronouncement, as described above, the tribunal described and evaluated the reports and testimony of each expert presented by both parties. It truly engaged with the scientific evidence.

The *Methanex* case is a comprehensive illustration of the involvement of expertise in a complex dispute. The procedural requirements for parties' written expert reports, oral testimony of such experts, challenges to party-appointed experts (or their reports), as well as judicial assessment of expert evidence – this case is an excellent example of all these stages of expert use in a dispute. Not only that, the award is a good illustration of the way a tribunal should engage with the evidence, with cogent reasoning for acceptance or rejection of the same.

5.2 *Detroit International Bridge Company v. Canada*

Detroit International Bridge Company v. Canada is a NAFTA arbitration using UNCITRAL Rules. It concerned the investment of an American company in the Ambassador Bridge over the Detroit River, connecting Detroit, Michigan in the United States and Windsor, Ontario in Canada. The Canadian government passed a law giving it authority over the construction, operation and

329 See, e.g., *id.*, paras. 98–100.
330 *Id.*, para. 101.

ownership of international bridges. This allegedly affected the bridge in which the claimant had invested.

The tribunal dismissed this case for lack of jurisdiction.[331] Nevertheless, it is interesting to note the provisions regarding the use of experts that the tribunal had laid down in its third procedural order. By Procedural Order No. 3, the tribunal noted that the disputing parties agreed on the provisions of the IBA Rules on the Taking of Evidence in International Arbitration, with respect to the presentation of expert witnesses[332] (among other provisions).[333]

Moreover, the tribunal further clarified with respect to expert witnesses, the procedure to be followed at oral hearings. This would involve direct examination by the appointing party, which would be followed by cross-examination by the opposing party and a final re-examination if the appointing party so wished, only it would be restricted to matters arising out of cross-examination. A further cross-examination could only be conducted with permission from the tribunal. The tribunal itself could examine the expert at any time during the above proceedings.[334] The tribunal could also at its discretion refuse to hear an expert or limit or refuse a party's right to examine an expert if it considers the expert's opinion irrelevant or opining on facts already proven. The tribunal could also call an expert for further examination at any time.[335] The above procedures are quite common and have been seen at the ICJ and before other tribunals as well.

Interestingly, this tribunal also explicitly stated that it would not be improper for counsel to meet potential experts to prepare expert statements and their oral examinations.[336] This is in consonance with the IBA Guidelines on Party Representation in International Arbitration which posit that there is nothing wrong in principle with the involvement of parties and counsel in drafting an expert opinion.[337]

---

331 *Detroit International Bridge Company v. The Government of Canada* (*Award on Jurisdiction*) (2 April 2015) PCA Case No. 2012–25, para. 340.

332 IBA Rules, *supra* note 315, arts. 4, 5.

333 *Detroit International Bridge Company v. Canada*, *supra* note 331, Procedural Order No. 2, para. 33.

334 *Id.*, paras. 50, 54.

335 *Id.*, paras. 52, 54.

336 *Id.*, paras. 53, 54.

337 IBA Guidelines on Party Representation in International Arbitration 2013, available at http://www.ibanet.org/Document/Default.aspx?DocumentUid=6F0C57D7-E7A0-43AF-B76E-714D9FE74D7F; accessed 20 June 2019, art. 24: 'A Party Representative may, consistent with the principle that the evidence given should reflect the Witness's own account of relevant facts, events or circumstances, or the Expert's own analysis or opinion, meet or interact with Witnesses and Experts in order to discuss and prepare their prospective testimony'.

Finally, after addressing party-appointed experts, the tribunal also noted its own power to appoint experts (or at a disputing party's request) to address one or more of the matters listed in NAFTA Article 1133. Such an appointment would only take place after consultation with the disputing parties on the selection, terms of reference and conclusions of any such expert. If the tribunal decides to take oral evidence from any such experts, the procedure governing party-appointed experts would apply to them as well.[338]

This case therefore, although marginally involving a river and substantively not relevant to international water law, is quite insightful from the perspective of procedures governing experts, as laid out by a NAFTA tribunal, operating under UNCITRAL Rules in conjunction with the NAFTA dispute resolution provisions. The oral procedures envisaged here are in consonance with those seen at the ICJ in recent times. The tribunal also incorporated guidelines that it found most useful from those found more commonly in international commercial arbitration (the IBA Guidelines). It shows that this tribunal made use of all procedural tools at its disposal, without restricting itself to the mandatory treaty provisions and rules by which it was bound.

5.3 *Bear Creek Mining Corporation v. Peru*

The *Bear Creek Mining Corporation v. Peru* dispute, under the Canada–Peru Free Trade Agreement (FTA), was arbitrated at ICSID. The claim arose out of a newly promulgated Peruvian law that revoked the claimant's concession to operate the Santa Ana mining project in Peru on the ground that it was no longer in the national interest, resulting in a complete cessation of activities at Santa Ana and alleged significant damages to the claimant. The case is relevant to this discussion given that one of the reasons for revocation of the license was safeguarding the people's right to water. The mining activity was feared to have been contaminating the nearby Desaguadero River and Lake Titicaca.

A large amount of expertise was used in this case in attempting to establish various kinds of facts. The claimant's memorial contained expert reports calculating the fair market value of the Santa Ana project, on Peruvian constitutional law, and on industry standards of environmental compliance by the Santa Ana project (the expert is a mining consultancy). It is interesting to note how the claimant drew out the credibility of the experts it used in its memorial. The valuation expert 'is a world-recognized leader in the field of forensic

338 *Detroit International Bridge Company v. Canada*, *supra* note 331, Procedural Order No. 2, para. 55.

accounting and damages valuation'.[339] One of the authors has extensive experience in the valuation and quantification of damages relating to mineral properties at all stages of development and served as an expert witness in over 200 quantification and valuation matters before courts and arbitral tribunals. The mining consultancy 'is widely recognized as the specialty firm of choice for resource and reserve work and has carried valuations of more than a thousand mineral exploration properties across the world over its nearly 30 years of existence'. This statement is followed by a description of the technical reviews and assessments carried out by this expert that are relevant to this dispute.[340]

The expert reports themselves, apart from their core content, included the qualifications of the experts and all sources of the information they relied on. The valuation expert report is more detailed, with curriculum vitae of the authors, the assumptions they made while carrying out their analysis, and an 'expert declaration' that may be termed as a statement of independence, though it is wider in scope, and akin to declarations required from experts under the ICJ Statute. It would have been useful to include such a declaration in other expert reports as well.

The respondent State also submitted expert reports in response to the above experts' reports. Their counter-memorial also countered the approach of the claimant's experts, in terms of valuation methodology and technical assumptions.[341] This was backed up by their own expert reports, with reasoning.

We see a similar reliance on fresh expert reports in the claimant's reply and respondent's rejoinder. Given the heavy reliance of parties on expert opinion, the tribunal also paid due attention to the handling of expert evidence during the oral proceedings.[342] The experts to be examined at the hearing were notified in advance. The order of expert testimony was divided by subject matter.[343] With respect to expert reports by multiple authors, each party was required to indicate which of the authors would be examined, keeping in mind that no more than two authors may be selected. The author(s) testifying must be able to answer questions related to the full report (whether in its entirety or in portions, as long as the full report was covered between them). If two experts tes-

339 *Bear Creek Mining Corporation v. Republic of Peru*, Claimant's Memorial on the Merits, ICSID Case No. ARB/14/21 (29 May 2015), para. 233.

340 *Id.*, paras. 233–234.

341 *Bear Creek Mining Corporation v. Republic of Peru*, Respondent's Counter-Memorial on the Merits and Memorial on Jurisdiction, ICSID Case No. ARB/14/21 (6 October 2015), paras. 15–18, 181, 340.

342 *Bear Creek Mining Corporation v. Republic of Peru*, Procedural Order No. 8, ICSID Case No. ARB/14/21 (4 August 2016).

343 *Id.*, para. 23.5.

tified regarding the same expert report, they were to testify at the same time. Finally, one of the two experts would be designated as the 'point person' to initially receive all questions and then decide which of the two testifying experts will answer. Only one expert could respond to each question posed.[344]

Interestingly, the tribunal also introduced the possibility of a method of expert examination that is infrequently used, that is, conferencing. The experts could be heard in this manner if the tribunal so wished after consulting with the parties.[345]

This tribunal also determined the maximum time period available to the parties for examination of witnesses and experts as 16.75 hours for each party.[346] This time included direct and re-examination of one's own expert and cross-examination of the opposing party's expert. Time spent on expert conferencing would be counted in half towards both parties' allocated time.[347] The time allocated for opening and closing statements could also be used for expert or witness examination, if left over. Declining to cross-examine an expert would not be deemed as acceptance of that expert's report.[348]

It is evident from reading the award that the tribunal engaged with and relied on parties' expert reports in reaching its conclusions, as did the partially dissenting arbitrator.[349] Procedurally, this tribunal too adhered to the IBA Rules as to the extent of the form of expert reports.[350] In terms of the procedure for examining experts, this ICSID tribunal naturally followed the ICSID arbitration rules on the subject. It further specified that experts may provide a brief presentation of the key points of their report of no longer than 30 minutes, except for experts on valuation of quantum of damages, who could take up to 45 minutes.[351] Cross-examination and re-examination would follow. Examination by video conference may be permitted for justified reasons at the discretion of the tribunal.[352] Other detailed rules on expert examination were in consonance with what is seen generally before other tribunals. A robust oral examination of experts is thus seen before this tribunal, including

344 *Id.*, para. 23.7.

345 *Id.*, para. 23.8.

346 *Id.*, para. 25.

347 *Id.*, para. 28.

348 *Id.*, para. 31.

349 *Bear Creek Mining Corporation v. Republic of Peru*, Partial Dissenting Opinion of Professor Philippe Sands, ICSID Case No. ARB/14/21 (30 November 2017).

350 *Bear Creek Mining Corporation v. Republic of Peru*, Procedural Order No. 1, ICSID Case No. ARB/14/21 (20 January 2015), para. 18.4.

351 *Id.*, para. 19.4.3.

352 *Id.*, para. 19.7.

innovative methods, which, though not unique, are not seen often in inter-state or investor-state disputes.

5.4 *Chevron v. Ecuador*

This dispute between Chevron and Ecuador, brought under the Ecuador–United States bilateral investment treaty, consisted of claims arising out of Texaco's historical activities under oil concession contracts and the alleged government misconduct in subsequent domestic litigation against Texaco for environmental remediation. The Ecuadorian government sought to protect the Amazon rainforest, namely, the Ecuadorian share of the Amazon River basin. The proceedings involved several phases and were conducted by the PCA with the UNCITRAL Arbitration Rules.

For the second partial award on Track II of this arbitration,[353] both parties engaged a large number of technical experts, as did the tribunal, on digital forensics. The claimants included 63 expert reports and the respondents 33 for this phase of the dispute alone. Three joint expert reports were also submitted.

A site visit was ordered by the tribunal and executed by the PCA Secretary-General, the parties, and the tribunal. The parties' legal representatives and experts addressed the tribunal at each of the four sites visited in Ecuador.[354]

By Procedural Order No. 26 and upon the terms set out there, the tribunal appointed a forensic expert. This expert's final report was sent to the parties who were invited to comment on it. Thereafter the expert's revised final report was sent to the parties and they were asked if they would like to question the tribunal's expert in an oral hearing. These were in consonance with the UNCITRAL Arbitration Rules. The parties waived their right to such a hearing.[355]

The tribunal expert attended the part of the Track II hearing where parties' experts gave short presentations and were cross-examined by opposing parties. The tribunal expert, however, did not provide oral or written evidence before the Tribunal then or later, apart from her final report and revised final report.[356] In accordance with Procedural Order No. 40, the tribunal expert considered the expert reports and oral testimony of the parties' experts in order to identify (i) any material points on which there was common ground between the technical testimony and conclusions of these experts, (ii) any mate-

353 *Chevron Corporation and Texaco Petroleum Company v. Republic of Ecuador* (*Second Partial Award on Track II*) (30 August 2018) PCA Case No. 2009–23.

354 *Id.*, para. 1.64.

355 *Id.*, paras. 1.26–1.43.

356 *Id.*, para. 6.4.

rial points of difference between their technical testimony and conclusions, (iii) whether the differences arose from a difference in technical analysis or whether they were attributable to non-technical facts, and (iv) any material conclusions put forward by the experts which she would not characterise as matters of technical analysis.[357]

Subsequent to the tribunal expert's draft report and discussions with the party-appointed experts, she prepared her final report.[358] The tribunal clarified that it had received no private advice from its appointed expert.[359] This seemingly innocuous statement is very important in terms of safeguarding parties' rights of due process and guarding against the use of phantom expertise, as mentioned in the context of the ICJ.

The tribunal was able to conclude from the expert reports of the parties and its own expert that there were few, if any, material differences between the expert witnesses in relation to the technical evidence. The various points of disagreement between the expert witnesses arose from significant differences in the way in which the party-appointed experts approached and interpreted that evidence based on their respective terms of reference.[360] This pronouncement also demonstrates the utility of using tribunal-appointed experts in drawing out the relevant points of difference between party-appointed experts. It also shows that party-appointed experts need not be biased in favour of their appointing party; their testimony in favour of the appointing party may be due to carefully crafted terms of reference provided by the same party.[361]

From the above description in Track II of the arbitration in *Chevron v. Ecuador*, we get a good understanding of how a tribunal functions with its own appointed expert, especially in a situation where party-appointed experts are also present. It is evident from a reading of the partial award that the tribunal engaged to a great extent with the voluminous expert evidence before it arrived at a reasoned decision.

5.5 *Disputes without the Involvement of Experts*

A few other investment arbitration disputes involving water resources are described briefly below, in order to illustrate those kinds of cases that involved complex facts and potentially would have benefited from expert use. The reason for the absence of experts in these cases is explored here.

357 *Id.*, para. 6.5.
358 *Id.*, para. 6.6.
359 *Id.*, para. 6.11.
360 *Id.*, paras. 6.12, 6.13.
361 *Id.*, para. 6.108: 'The eventual differences between the two experts are more differences of perspective, also influenced by non-technical factors lying outside their expert functions in this arbitration and influenced their respective terms of reference from the Parties'.

5.5.1 Salini v. Jordan

In *Salini v. Jordan*, arbitrated under the Italy–Jordan bilateral investment treaty, involved claims arising out of the disagreement between the government of Jordan and the investor Salini as to the amount owed to the claimants for works done under a contract for the construction of a dam over the River Jordan, in Jordan.[362]

The claimant's primary argument in this case hinged on the validity of an oral agreement that Italy (the claimant's state of nationality) entered into with the respondent to submit this dispute to arbitration.[363] The tribunal found that the claimants had failed to prove that a binding agreement had been orally concluded between Italy and Jordan.[364] Hence, it was not necessary to proceed to consider the merits of the case. As a result, the question of involvement of experts in resolving the dispute did not arise in this case.

5.5.2 Bayview Irrigation District, et al. v. United Mexican States

The *Bayview Irrigation District et al. v. Mexico* dispute arose after Mexico captured and diverted irrigation water for Mexican farm use, allegedly depriving an investor of its rights to import a portion of waters from Rio Grande tributaries to the United States. However, the case did not proceed since the tribunal found as a preliminary matter that Chapter 11 of NAFTA was not intended to provide substantive protections or rights of action to investors whose investments were wholly confined to their home state territory.[365] Thus, the investment was not 'international' enough to attract the provisions of NAFTA.[366]

The claim had alleged that Mexico violated the 1944 Treaty by constructing and operating seven dams on the tributaries of the Rio Grande that are collecting and diverting water for use by its own nationals, water rights belonging to the claimants, thus increasing the deficit flow to the claimants. They also estimated the economic value of their irrigation water in the lower Rio Grande Valley from 1992 to 2002, and the interest owed on that amount. Had this case reached the merits phase, it might have involved technical facts that would benefit from expert assistance.

---

362 *Salini Costruttori S.pA and Italstrade S.pA v. Hashemite Kingdom of Jordan*, ICSID Case No. ARB/02/13 (31 January 2006).

363 *Id.*, para. 43.

364 *Id.*, para. 100.

365 *Bayview Irrigation District et al. v. United Mexican States*, ICSID Case No. ARB(AF)/05/1 (19 June 2007).

366 Boisson de Chazournes, *supra* note 44, at 226.

5.5.3 Vattenfall v. Germany

This dispute arose under the Energy Charter Treaty, when Vattenfall, a Swedish energy company, initiated a claim against Germany over permit delays for a coal-fired power plant in Hamburg.[367] The delays were linked with opposition to the plant on environmental grounds and additional requirements to protect the Elbe River, subsequent to a domestic court decision. The investor-state dispute arose directly out of these environmental requirements to protect the river, which the claimant deemed as unlawful expropriation and a violation of Germany's obligation to afford foreign investors 'fair and equitable treatment'.

A dispute of this nature was ideal for the involvement of technical expertise to examine the need for additional clearances to protect the Elbe River. However, the parties reached a settlement instead of proceeding with the arbitration, and the outcome was that the government was obliged to drop its additional environmental requirements and issue the contested permits required for the plant to proceed. Unfortunately, Vattenfall's earlier commitments to mitigate the coal plant's impact on the Elbe River were also waived through this settlement.[368]

Part 6: Conclusion: Assessment of the Use of Experts in International Water Disputes

6.1 *General Trends in Expert Use*

The examination of case law throughout this monograph has shown greater absence than use of experts. That in itself points towards a few conclusions. Overall, there are two kinds of disputes that have seen absence of experts. The first is where there is genuinely no need for involving experts, the dispute being resolved solely through application of legal principles or the relevant facts or parameters that are spelt out in a legal instrument. The second is the category of cases which have received strong criticism for either not involving experts or for engaging phantom experts.

It is useful to compare this latter category with cases where experts are involved, but the court or tribunal does not engage with them. There is not much practical difference between these and the previous category of cases where experts are absent. Thus, it is not only important to have experts present in some capacity, they and their opinions need to be substantively used by the adjudicator in order to either accept or reject the evidence.

367 *Vattenfall AB, Vattenfall Europe AG, Vattenfall Europe Generation AG v Federal Republic of Germany* ICSID Case No. ARB/09/6 (11 March 2011).

368 *Id.*, paras. 12–13.

A small but growing number of cases involve experts, which are effectively used by the adjudicator in decision-making. Such cases truly demonstrate how experts can be extremely useful and sometimes indispensable in deciding international disputes, especially those relating to freshwater. The preceding analysis has also shown that these experts may be present in various forms – party-appointed, court-appointed, or a part of the tribunal itself, or sometimes even the sole determinant in a dispute.

Overall, it is the authors' opinion that experts are needed more than they are used today. Many of the cases examined in this monograph had experts involved in some form or another, or not at all. The case analysis has, however, revealed that the court or tribunal could have used experts for better implementation of the judgment or for bringing greater legitimacy to the decision. It is not, however, the authors' perspective that all technical issues in a dispute necessitate a tribunal's appointment of experts. Often, if the case involves party-appointed experts, as demonstrated by a few previous decisions, the agreement of opposing party experts or when a party does not dispute the other party's evidence, party-appointed experts seem to suffice.

6.2 *Specific Trends in Different Fora*

6.2.1 At the ICJ

A number of common threads emerge from the above assessment of disputes involving scientific issues before the ICJ. First, it is easily observed that experts may be involved in different ways in a dispute, either as counsel for a party, an expert witness or, less frequently, court-appointed. In spite of the long history of expert involvement as counsel, it is now no longer encouraged in light of the *Pulp Mills* decision. Thus, it is more useful for parties to bring experts to testify in the oral proceedings if they wish to produce experts at all. The ICJ has generally preferred that the parties engage their own experts and present their findings to the Court.[369] In boundary disputes in particular, the absence of court-appointed experts is strongly felt. Disputes that did involve court-appointed experts, whether appointed of the Court's own accord, or at the request of parties, have been resolved to the satisfaction of the parties. Where the Court did not overtly appoint experts, it has been criticized for not doing so, either by dissenting judges, or in scholarly opinion. This criticism has extended to those situations where the Court seems to have resorted to the assistance of phantom experts. Commentators have found it indefensible for the Court 'to have recourse to an invisible genre of experts, instead of resorting to transparent, institutionalized mechanisms for the consultation of expertise

369 M. Bennouna, *'Experts before the International Court of Justice: What For?'*, 9 Journal of International Dispute Settlement (2018) 345–351, at 346.

relevant to the case at hand'.[370] Without the parties' opportunity to comment on the expert opinion, risks of technical errors increase.[371]

A further resource statutorily at the Court's disposal is the appointment of assessors,[372] a tool that the ICJ has never used in water disputes or otherwise.[373] On some occasions, especially at the final stage of the Court's deliberations,[374] these may be a simpler alternative to Article 50 experts, and more transparent than phantom experts. Assessors participate in the Court's deliberations without the right to vote.[375] The absence of assessors in the Court's practice may be in part due to the perception of the excessive influence on the judges and thereby the outcome of the dispute, since they take part in the deliberations. Moreover, parties are not required to be informed or given the opportunity to comment on the opinions or advice of the assessors. These opinions would not be treated as evidence before the Court.[376] Thus, due process concerns arise from this restriction on the parties' right to comment.[377] The selection of assessors, statutorily, does not seem to involve parties either. However, it has been argued that Article 9(2) of the Rules of Court could be interpreted to include the view of the parties within 'information relevant the choice of assessors'.[378]

Nevertheless, there are several advantages to the use of assessors. They provide judges with the necessary technical knowledge to effectively address the subject matter of the issues in dispute. They may also enhance the authority and legitimacy of the judgment by increasing the perception that the facts underlying the dispute have been assessed accurately and diligently.[379] Assessors could perform the same function as phantom experts; but compared to invisible experts, they would have the advantage of offering a more transparent contribution to the work of the ICJ.[380]

370 Peat, *supra* note 84, at 300.

371 Coustasse & Sweeney-Samuelson, *supra* note 103, at 468–469.

372 See Part 3; Riddell, *supra* note 78, at 253.

373 Although, see *Delimitation of the Maritime Boundary in the Gulf of Maine Area (Canada/United States of America)*, Judgment, ICJ Reports 1984, 246, where the expert appointed by the Court at the parties' joint request was said to be akin to an assessor.

374 G. Gaja, *'Assessing Expert Evidence in the ICJ'*, 15:3 The Law & Practice of International Courts and Tribunals (2016) 409–418, at 417.

375 *Id.*

376 *Id.*, at 417–418.

377 *Id.*

378 L. C. Lima, *'Expert Advisor or Non-Voting Adjudicator? The Potential Function of Assessors in the Procedure of the International Court of Justice'*, 4 Rivista di Diritto Internazionale (2016) 1123–1146, at 1129.

379 On the issue of legitimacy see T. Treves, *'Aspects of Legitimacy of Decisions of International Courts and Tribunals'*, in R. Wolfrum & V. Röben (eds.), *Legitimacy in International Law* (Berlin, Heidelberg: Springer, 2008) 169–188.

380 Lima, *supra* note 378, at 1134.

The presence of the parties' experts does not automatically obviate the need for Court-appointed experts. Of course there may be situations where expert evidence and expert opinion from parties resolve certain scientific issues or the dispute entirely. Such situations may arise when experts of opposing parties agree. However, the question then arises as to whether it is a Court's task to objectively assess the facts or to accept something as a fact merely because both parties agree.

It is also not obligatory for the Court to unquestioningly accept the opinion of an expert it appoints.[381] The appointment of an expert by the Court has its own merits, as noted by Judge Yusuf:

> It cannot be expected that expert opinions or scientific assessments commissioned by the Court will always arrive at uniform conclusions, but the adversarial process by which the Parties are given an opportunity to comment on such opinions provides the Court with further insight into the relevance and significance not only of the factual material presented by the Parties, but of the expert opinion as well. Moreover, the use of an enquiry or an expert report by the Court has the advantage of enhancing the confidence of the Parties in the technical evaluation by the Court of the factual and scientific information provided by them and ensuring transparency.[382]

It is important that the Court assesses the scientific evidence rather than avoiding it by using legal arguments. To avoid examining these issues, the Court can find that the parties appeared to agree on certain matters or that some evidence was uncontested.[383] Alternatively, the Court has observed that one of the parties (generally the applicant) failed to provide sufficient evidence to sustain its claims.[384] However, the methods of avoiding a decision on scientific or technical matters are not always available or appropriate. In the event that resolving a scientific or technical question is necessary to deciding a dispute,

381 M. Lachs, *'Evidence in the Procedure of the International Court of Justice: Role of the Court'*, in E. Bello & Prince B. Ajibola (eds.), *Essays in Honour of Judge Taslim Olawale Elias*, vol. II (Leiden: Martinus Nijhoff, 1992) at 273, cited in Riddell & Plant, *supra* note 55, at 334: 'how far the Court should rely on ... experts is a question of discretion'.

382 *Pulp Mills*, Yusuf, *supra* note 123, at 217.

383 *Kasikili/Sedudu Island*, Judgment, *supra* note 88, at 1096; see also *Whaling in the Antarctic* (*Australia v. Japan: New Zealand intervening*), Judgment, ICJ Reports 2014 226, 258.

384 *Pulp Mills*, Judgment, *supra* note 116, at 94, 97–101; *Certain Activities and Construction of a Road*, Judgment, *supra* note 145, at 68, 71–73.

the Court needs to find ways to attain the knowledge required to address scientific or technical issues.[385]

It is not the authors' submission that all disputes of a scientific nature, whether or not involving parties' experts, should involve Court-appointed experts. It has been seen in a few of the cases discussed above that the Court has avoided the need for assessing scientific evidence by emphasizing the legal aspect of a dispute and using only legal principles to arrive at a decision. Whether the Court is justified in doing so, and whether it is fulfilling its judicial function in this manner, may depend on the facts of the case. It is also useful to compare this with the approaches of other international tribunals.

6.2.2 International Arbitration

The diverse examples of arbitrations conducted in varied fora highlights the equally diverse ways in which arbitral tribunals have used experts. While some cases were resolved with parties' experts or expert reports alone, others saw the tribunal appointing its own experts. A new form of expert assistance is the incorporation of expertise into the tribunal. Apart from the specific situation envisaged in the Indus Waters Treaty, with a seven-member tribunal, it should be relatively simple to include an expert (non-legal) adjudicator into a tribunal in those contexts where relevant treaties or rules do not specify legal qualifications for an arbitrator.

Certain qualities have been considered indispensable in an arbitrator, namely, the ability to manage the proceedings; to understand the nature of the technical issues and the substance of the dispute between the parties; to understand the law and apply it to the substance of the dispute; to reach, as far as possible, a consensus with the co-arbitrators (except in the case of a sole arbitrator); and to write an enforceable award.[386] Even if the expert is unable to fulfil all of these requirements, the tribunal as a whole, composed of legal experts as well, should be able to do so. Some concerns arise, however, where there are one or two expert arbitrators out of a tribunal of three. Selecting an expert arbitrator based on industry expertise is feared to bring in a bias borne out of the expertise gained working on one side or the other of a relevant issue.[387] With an even number of expert arbitrators in an odd-numbered tribunal, there may be conflicting scientific opinions on the tribunal, leading to a problem similar to party-appointed experts. If the dispute also includes party-appointed

385 Gaja, *supra* note 374, at 411.

386 P. S. Caldwell, *'Is Procedural Warfare Sidelining Subject Matter Expertise?'*, 14 Transnational Dispute Management (2017), available at http://www.transnational-dispute-management.com/article.asp?key=2446.

387 C. J. Moxley, Jr., *'Selecting the Ideal Arbitrator'*, 60:3 Dispute Resolution Journal (2005) 1–6, at 4.

experts, there may be more than two differing opinions to contend with, since there is no guarantee they would agree on any issue between themselves, or indeed that their views would coincide with those of the co-arbitrators.[388] Yet, if the *Kishenganga* decision is any indication, the use of a technical arbitrator in a tribunal could positively influence the tribunal and improve the quality of decision-making. The above-mentioned problems could be resolved by limiting the number of expert arbitrators to one (or an odd number on a larger tribunal) and not having one serve as the tribunal president.[389]

The expert member of the tribunal in the *Kishenganga* arbitration noted the value of integrating an expert as a member of an adjudicative body. Such an expert may facilitate other members' understanding of the issues, undertake technical analysis, assist colleagues in weighing the credibility of scientific evidence, and check facts and analysis. In his opinion, access to independent scientific advice by means of experts that sat alongside court members could prove useful.[390]

In an expert report, the expert's choice of methodology should be supported by authoritative treatises, guidelines or similar sources. In the absence of such sources, it would be useful to find a consensus within the relevant community of experts regarding the reliability of the chosen methodology and the appropriateness of applying it in the circumstances. If most experts in the field would ordinarily use a different methodology and arrive at a different conclusion, this is likely to cast serious doubts on the credibility of the expert's report.[391] The IBA Rules also provide useful guidance on the contents of an expert report.[392] One of its inclusions, the terms of reference of the expert, should be described clearly, since it would be vital to the tribunal's understanding of the scope of the expert's work, and allow the opposing party's expert to properly respond to the first report.[393] The expert's factual assumptions should also feature in addition to the terms of reference, which made it easier to distinguish the expert's opinion from fact (or assumed fact) and to identify the situations that have or have not been considered by the expert.[394] A further integral part of the report is the explanation of the methodology employed by the expert and

388 E. E. Triantafilou, *'Non-Lawyer Arbitrators and the Deliberative Balance of International Arbitral Tribunals'*, (2) Transnational Dispute Management (2017) at 6.

389 *Id.*, at 9.

390 Keene, *supra* note 248, at 255.

391 D. Roney, *'Cross-Examination of Experts'*, in S. Jagusch QC, P. Pinsolle & A. G. Leventhal (eds.), *The Guide to Advocacy*, 3rd edition (London: Global Arbitration Review, 2018).

392 IBA Rules, *supra* note 315, art. 5.2.

393 N. Blackaby & A. Wilbraham, *'Practical Issues Relating to the Use of Expert Evidence in Investment Treaty Arbitration'*, 31:3 ICSID Review (2016) 655–669, at 659.

394 *Id.*

the documents relied on. This makes it independently verifiable and susceptible to peer review.[395]

The court or tribunal should also provide some guidance to the parties as to the issues they wish to be addressed in the respective reports. Often, tribunals are faced with reports containing independent methodologies, divergent conclusions, and are of little value to the adjudicator to resolve a scientific issue.[396]

Counsel collaboration in drafting expert reports (or their refinement) is considered an inescapable reality of arbitration proceedings (as well as other judicial proceedings).[397] While some international guidelines provide for disclosure of counsel-expert communication, many do not find this advisable, noting instead that unconstrained collaboration between counsel and experts positively affects the quality of representation provided to the party and the quality and accessibility of the expert evidence submitted to the tribunal. It also increases efficiency and reduces the cost of proceedings without altering the independence of the expert.[398] This perspective finds no danger of the expert becoming an advocate for the party in this way and places its trust in the tribunal's wisdom to identify such tainted reports.[399]

To respect due process, parties should be involved in every stage of the tribunal expert's work and receive copies of and have an opportunity to comment on the expert's work product.[400] If the expert conducts site visits, parties or their representatives should be permitted to be present there as well, to the extent that they do not interfere with the expert's work.

It is important to carefully define the terms of reference of the tribunal's expert. The UNCITRAL Notes on Organizing Arbitral Proceedings are a useful

395 *Id.*, at 660.

396 K. Sachs & N. Schmidt-Ahrendts, *'Protocol on Expert Teaming: A New Approach to Expert Evidence'*, in A. J. van den Berg (ed.), *Arbitration Advocacy in Changing Times*, ICCA Congress Series, 2010 Rio Volume 15 (Alphen aan den Rijn: Kluwer Law International, 2011), 135–148, paras. 21–23; J. Waincymer, 'Chapter 12: General Witness and Expert Evidence', *Procedure and Evidence in International Arbitration* (Alphen aan den Rijn: Kluwer Law International, 2012) at 933.

397 K. Parlett, *'Parties' Engagement with Experts in International Litigation'*, 9:3 Journal of International Dispute Settlement (2018) 440–452, at 447.

398 P. D. Friedland & K. Brown de Vejar, *'Discoverability of Communications Between Counsel and Party-Appointed Experts in International Arbitration'*, in A. J. van den Berg (ed.), *Arbitration Advocacy in Changing Times*, ICCA Congress Series, 2010 Rio Volume 15 (Alphen aan den Rijn: Kluwer Law International, 2011) 160–180, at 177–178.

399 *Id.*

400 C. von Wobeser, *'The Arbitral Tribunal-Appointed Expert'*, in A. J. van den Berg (ed.), *International Arbitration 2006: Back to Basics?*, ICCA Congress Series, 2006 Montreal Volume 13 (Alphen aan den Rijn: Kluwer Law International, 2007) 801–812, at 811.

guide in this respect.[401] The parties should be involved in the preparation of the terms of reference given that they can make very valuable contributions in identifying the points to be resolved by the expert and the possible obstacles that may have to be confronted.[402] The terms of reference or questions put to the experts should not indicate the tribunal's perspective on the issue; there should be no leading questions. While this may seem quite evident in domestic proceedings in common law countries, the same is not universally known, and not included in any statutes or rules for the major international fora. Whether the expert should have access to the parties' submissions depends on the nature and scope of the expert's work. At times it is prudent for the expert to have all the case material at her disposal, at other times, when the tribunal is only seeking answers to specific questions, it may be beneficial for the expert to work in a vacuum.

The expert's final report should indicate if either of the parties or a third party did not provide the information requested and, to the extent possible, the causes for not doing so.[403] It is advisable for the expert's final report to contain his or her relationship with any of the parties or arbitrators, curriculum vitae, credentials as an expert, and copies of documents, graphs, photographs or videos relied on in the report. In essence, the expert's report should correspond to a party-appointed expert's report in form. Thus, assumptions made and the methodology followed necessarily should be included apart from the conclusions reached.[404] In the event that a tribunal wishes to seek further assistance from the expert during deliberations, due process demands that the parties remain informed of the tribunal and expert's exchanges, and that they have an opportunity to comment on the expert's responses.[405] Notwithstanding the right to comment in writing, the right of the parties to request a hearing to listen to and question the tribunal's expert should be recognized, as the majority of arbitration rules do. The arbitral tribunal, depending on the circumstances of the case, should conduct the hearing in a manner so as to best illuminate the expert evidence, such as by permitting parties to bring their own experts to the hearing to pose questions to the tribunal's expert.[406] In this manner, by

401 See discussion of Article 16(a)(i) in United Nations Commission on International Trade Law (UNCITRAL), *UNCITRAL Notes on Organizing Arbitral Proceedings* (New York: United Nations, 2012) para. 71 at 25, available at http://www.uncitral.org/pdf/english/texts/arbitration/arb-notes/arb-notes-e.pdf; accessed 30 January 2019.

402 von Wobeser, *supra* note 400, at 809–810.

403 *Id.*, at 810.

404 *Id.*, at 810–811.

405 Waincymer, *supra* note 396, at 949.

406 von Wobeser, *supra* note 400, at 811.

tribunals learning best practices from each other, or even from other dispute settlement fora, the settlement of water disputes could be enhanced through effective utilization of expert opinion.

Acknowledgements

The authors would like to extend their sincere thanks and appreciation to Dr. Salman M. A. Salman, Editor-in-Chief, for his constant support and enthusiasm, as well as the excellent advice throughout the preparation and finalization of the present monograph. Our thanks and appreciation are also due to the anonymous reviewers, as well as the members of the Editorial Board of *Brill Research Perspectives in International Water Law*, for overseeing the review process, and for the helpful and constructive comments on the monograph.

Author Biographies

Makane Moïse Mbengue
is Professor of International Law at the Faculty Law and the Institute of Environmental Sciences of the University of Geneva, and Affiliate Professor at Sciences Po Paris (School of Law). He has acted and acts as expert for the Senegal River Development Organization (OMVS), the Niger Basin Authority, the Lake Chad Commission, the Nile River Basin Initiative and the World Bank in the field of water law. He is one of the co-editors of the Oxford Commentary on the 1997 United Nations Convention on the Law of Non-Navigational Uses of International Watercourses. He has published extensively in the field of international water law, as well as on the topic of experts before international courts and tribunals.

Rukmini Das
is a PhD candidate at the Faculty of Law, University of Geneva. Her subject of research is 'Scientific Experts in International Disputes.' She also recently completed work on a research project on 'Experts and International Courts and Tribunals', funded by the Swiss National Science Foundation, along with a number of publications on the same subject.

Bibliography

Anders Ericsson, K., N. Charness, R. R. Hoffman & P. J. Feltovich (eds.), *The Cambridge Handbook of Expertise and Expert Performance* (Cambridge: Cambridge University Press, 2006).

Bennouna, M., *'Experts before the International Court of Justice: What For?'*, 9 Journal of International Dispute Settlement (2018) 345–351.

Blackaby, N., & A. Wilbraham, *'Practical Issues Relating to the Use of Expert Evidence in Investment Treaty Arbitration'*, 31:3 ICSID Review (2016) 655–669.

Bogdanović, S., *'The International Law Association Helsinki Rules'*, 3:4 Brill Research Perspectives in International Water Law (2018) 1–110.

Boisson de Chazournes, L., *Fresh Water in International Law* (Oxford: Oxford University Press, 2013).

Bolivian Thoughts, 'Bolivian Team Presents Study on The Origin of Silala Waters' (14 February 2018), available at http://bolivianthoughts.com/2018/02/16/bolivian-team-presents-study-on-the-origin-of-silala-waters-chile-to-face-a-defeat-and-ridicule/; accessed 20 June 2019.

Bourne, C. B., *'The International Law Association's Contribution to International Water Resources Law'*, 36 Natural Resources Journal (1996) 155–216.

Boyle, A., 'Environmental Dispute Settlement', *Max Planck Encyclopedia of Public International Law* (Oxford: Oxford University Press, 2009).

Boyle, A., & J. Harrison, *'Judicial Settlement of International Environmental Disputes: Current Problems'*, 4 Journal of International Dispute Settlement (2013) 245–276.

Caldwell, P. S., *'Is Procedural Warfare Sidelining Subject Matter Expertise?'*, 14 Transnational Dispute Management (2017), available at http://www.transnational-dispute-management.com/article.asp?key=2446.

Coustasse, J. G. S., & E. Sweeney-Samuelson, *'Adjudicating Conflicts over Resources: The ICJ's Treatment of Technical Evidence in the Pulp Mills Case'*, 3 Goettingen Journal of International Law (2011) 447–471.

Couvreur P., *'Le Règlement Juridictionnel'*, in Institut du Droit Economique de la Mer (ed.), *Le processus de délimitation maritime: étude d'un cas fictif. Colloque international de Monaco du 27 au 29 mars 2003* (Paris: Pedone, 2004) 349–388.

Crook, J. R., *'In Re Indus Waters Kishenganga Arbitration (Pakistan v. India)'*, 108:2 American Journal of International Law (2014) 308–314.

Fach Gómez, K., *'The US-EU Transatlantic Trade and Investment Partnership: Should It Leave a Door Open for Non-Legal Arbitrators?'*, 34:2 Conflict Resolution Quarterly (2016) 189–223.

Foster, C. E., *Science and the Precautionary Principle in International Courts and Tribunals: Expert Evidence, Burden of Proof and Finality* (Cambridge: Cambridge University Press, 2011).

Friedland, P. D., & K. Brown de Vejar, *'Discoverability of Communications between Counsel and Party-Appointed Experts in International Arbitration'*, in A. J. van den Berg (ed.), *Arbitration Advocacy in Changing Times*, ICCA Congress Series, 2010 Rio Volume 15 (Alphen aan den Rijn: Kluwer Law International, 2011) 160–180.

Gaja, G., *'Assessing Expert Evidence in the ICJ'*, 15:3 The Law & Practice of International Courts and Tribunals (2016) 409–418.

Hodgson, M., & M. Stewart, 'Experts in Investor-State Arbitration: The Tribunal as Gatekeeper', 9:3 Journal of International Dispute Settlement (2018) 453–463.

International Law Association, 'The Helsinki Rules on the Uses of the Waters of International Rivers', in *Report of the Fifty-Second Conference* (Helsinki, 1966).

Jennings, Sir R., *'International Lawyers and the Progressive Development of International Law'*, in J. Makarczyk (ed.), *Theory of International Law at the Threshold of the 21st Century: Essays in Honour of Krzysztof Skubiszewski* (Leiden: Martinus Nijhoff, 1996) 413–424.

Keene, A., *'Outcome Paper for the Seminar on the International Court of Justice at 70: In Retrospect and in Prospect'*, 7:2 Journal of International Dispute Settlement (2016) 238–265.

Lachs, M., 'Evidence in the Procedure of the International Court of Justice: Role of the Court', in E. Bello & Prince B. Ajibola (eds.), *Essays in Honour of Judge Taslim Olawale Elias*, vol. II (Leiden: Martinus Nijhoff, 1992).

Lador, Y., 'Access to Justice and Public Participation in the Water Sector: A Promising Legal Development', in M. Tignino & K. Sangbana (eds.), *Public Participation and Water Resources Management: Where Do We Stand in International Law? International Conference, Geneva 13 December 2013, Proceedings* (Paris: UNESCO, 2015) 147–153.

Lamb, S. J., S. M. Pape & L. Hamzi, *'Procedural Issues'*, in J. A. Trenor (ed.), *The Guide to Damages in International Arbitration*, 2nd edition (London: Global Arbitration Review, 2016) 107–122.

Lima, L. C., *'Expert Advisor or Non-Voting Adjudicator? The Potential Function of Assessors in the Procedure of the International Court of Justice'*, 4 Rivista di Diritto Internazionale (2016) 1123–1146.

Lorenzmeier, S., 'Indus Water Kishenganga Arbitration (Pakistan v. India)', *Max Planck Encyclopedia of Public International Law* (Oxford: Oxford University Press, 2015).

Ma, X., *'Introducing Non-Legal Adjudicators as a Counterbalanced Measure for Non-Appearance in Inter-State Adjudication and Arbitration'*, 14:2 Transnational Dispute Management (2017) 1–23.

Mbengue, M. M., *'International Courts and Tribunals as Fact-Finders: The Case of Scientific Fact-Finding in International Adjudication'*, 34:1 Loyola of Los Angeles International and Comparative Law Review (2011) 53–80.

McCaffrey, S. C., *The Law of International Watercourses*, 3rd edition (Oxford: Oxford University Press, 2019).

Meshel, T., *'What's in a Name? The Silala Waters and the Applicability of International Watercourse Law'*, 39 Questions of International Law (2017) 5–22.

Moxley, Jr., C. J., *'Selecting the Ideal Arbitrator'*, 90:3 Dispute Resolution Journal (2005) 1–6.

Parlett, K., *'Parties' Engagement with Experts in International Litigation'*, 9:3 Journal of International Dispute Settlement (2018) 440–452.

Peat, D., *'The Use of Court-Appointed Experts by the International Court of Justice'*, 84:1 British Yearbook of International Law (2014) 271–303.

Proposals for Amendment of the ICSID Rules, Working Paper No. 2, Vol. 1 (March 2019).

Riddell, A., *'Scientific Evidence in the International Court of Justice: Problems and Possibilities'*, 20 Finnish Yearbook of International Law (2009) 229–258.

Riddell, A., & B. Plant, *Evidence Before the International Court of Justice* (London: British Institute for International and Comparative Law, 2009).

Roney, D., *'Cross-Examination of Experts'*, in S. Jagusch QC, P. Pinsolle & A. G. Leventhal (eds.), *The Guide to Advocacy*, 3rd edition (London: Global Arbitration Review, 2018).

Rosenne, S., *Procedure in the International Court: A Commentary on the 1978 Rules of the International Court of Justice* (Leiden: Martinus Nijhoff, 1983).

Rudall, J., *'Certain Activities Carried Out by Nicaragua in the Border Area (Costa Rica v. Nicaragua)'*, 112:2 American Journal of International Law (2018) 288–294.

Sachs, K. & N. Schmidt-Ahrendts, *'Protocol on Expert Teaming: A New Approach to Expert Evidence'*, in A. J. van den Berg (ed.), *Arbitration Advocacy in Changing Times*, ICCA Congress Series, 2010 Rio Volume 15 (Alphen aan den Rijn: Kluwer Law International, 2011), 135–148.

Salman, S. M. A., *'International Water Disputes: A New Breed of Claims, Claimants, and Settlement Institutions'*, 31:1 Water International (2006) 2–11.

Salman, S. M. A., *'The United Nations Watercourses Convention Ten Years Later: Why Has Its Entry into Force Proven Difficult?'*, 32:1 Water International (2007) 1–15.

Salman, S. M. A., *'The Abyei Territorial Dispute between North and South Sudan: Why Has Its Resolution Proven Difficult?'*, in J. Unruh & R. C. Williams (eds.), *Land and Post-Conflict Peacebuilding* (Abingdon: Routledge, 2013) 25–68.

Salman, S. M. A., *'International Rivers as Boundaries: The Dispute over Kasikili/Sedudu Island and the Decision of the International Court of Justice'*, 25:4 Water International (2000) 580–585.

Salman, S. M. A., *'The Baglihar Difference and Its Resolution Process – A Triumph for the Indus Waters Treaty?'*, 10:2 Water Policy (2008) 105–117.

Salman, S. M. A., *'The Obligation Not to Cause Significant Harm (Article 7)'*, in L. Boisson de Chazournes, M. Moïse Mbengue, M. Tignino, K. Sangbana & J. Rudall (eds.),

The UN Convention on the Law of the Non-Navigational Uses of International Watercourses: A Commentary (Oxford: Oxford University Press, 2019) 95–122.

Salman, S. M. A., & K. Uprety, *Conflict and Cooperation on South Asia's International Rivers: A Legal Perspective* (Alphen aan den Rijn: Kluwer Law International, 2002).

Salman, S. M. A., & K. Uprety, *'Shared Watercourses and Water Security in South Asia: Challenges of Negotiating and Enforcing Treaties'*, 3:3 Brill Research Perspectives in International Water Law (2018) 1–100.

Salmon, J., *Dictionnaire de droit international public* (Brussels: Emile Bruylant, 2001).

Sands, P., 'Watercourses, Environment and International Court of Justice: The Gabčíkovo-Nagymaros Case', in S. M. A. Salman & L. Boisson de Chazournes (eds.), *International Watercourses: Enhancing Cooperation and Managing Conflict* (Washington, DC: The World Bank, 1998) 103–126.

Sands, P., *'Water and International Law: Science and Evidence in International Litigation'*, 22:4 Environmental Law and Management (2010) 151–161.

Schofield, C., & C. Carleton, *'Technical Considerations in Law of the Sea Dispute Resolution'*, in A. G. Oude Elferink & D. R. Rothwell (eds.), *Oceans Management in the 21st Century: Institutional Frameworks and Responses* (Leiden: Martinus Nijhoff, 2004) 231–254.

Sidhu, B., *'The Kishenganga Arbitration: Transboundary Water Resources Governance'*, 43:3 Environmental Policy and Law (2013) 147–161.

Talmon, S., *'Article 43'*, in A. Zimmermann, C. Tomuschat & K. Oellers-Frahm (eds.), *The Statute of the International Court of Justice: A Commentary*, 1st edition (Oxford: Oxford University Press, 2006) 977–1038.

Tams, C. J., *'Article 50'*, in A. Zimmermann, C. Tomuschat & K. Oellers-Frahm (eds.), *The Statute of the International Court of Justice: A Commentary*, 1st edition (Oxford: Oxford University Press, 2006) 1109–1118.

Tanzi, A., & G. M. Farnelli *'The Settlement of Disputes through Non-Judicial Means (Article 33(1)–33(9))'*, in L. Boisson de Chazournes, M. Moïse Mbengue, M. Tignino, K. Sangbana & J. Rudall (eds.), *The UN Convention on the Law of the Non-Navigational Uses of International Watercourses: A Commentary* (Oxford: Oxford University Press, 2019) 349–363.

Thirlway, H., *'Article 30'*, in A. Zimmerman, C. Tomuschat & K. Oellers-Frahm (eds.), *The Statute of the International Court of Justice: A Commentary*, 1st edition (Oxford: Oxford University Press, 2006) 481–494.

Thomson, L. G. J., *'The ICJ and the Case Concerning the Gabčíkovo-Nagymaros Project: The Implications for International Watercourses Law and International Environmental Law'*, 3 Centre for Energy, Petroleum, Mineral Law and Policy Annual Review (1999) Article 8.

Tignino, M., 'Le fleuve Indus et ses usages: L'arbitrage relatif aux eaux du fleuve Kishenganga', 60 Annuaire français de droit international (2014) 519–542.

Tignino, M., *'Quasi-Judicial Bodies'*, in C. M. Brölmann & Y. Radi (eds.), *Research Handbook on the Theory and Practice of International Law-Making* (Cheltenham: Edward Elgar Publishing, 2016) 242–261.

Tomka, P., *'The First Site Visit of the International Court of Justice in Fulfilment of Its Judicial Function'*, 92:1 American Journal of International Law (1998) 133–140.

Treves, T., *'Aspects of Legitimacy of Decisions of International Courts and Tribunals'*, in R. Wolfrum & V. Röben (eds.), *Legitimacy in International Law* (Berlin, Heidelberg: Springer, 2008) 169–188.

Triantafilou, E. E., *'Non-Lawyer Arbitrators and the Deliberative Balance of International Arbitral Tribunals'*, 2 Transnational Dispute Management (2017).

United Nations Commission on International Trade Law (UNCITRAL), *UNCITRAL Notes on Organizing Arbitral Proceedings* (New York: United Nations, 2012).

United Nations Economic Commission for Europe (UNECE), Meeting of the Parties to the Convention on the Protection and Use of Transboundary Watercourses and International Lakes, 'Amendment to Articles 25 and 26 of the Convention', UN Doc ECE/MP.WAT/14 (12 January 2004) (entered into force 6 February 2013).

UNECE, 'Guidance Document on the Aarhus Convention Compliance Mechanism', available at http://www.unece.org/fileadmin/DAM/env/pp/compliance/CC_GuidanceDocument.pdf; accessed 21 July 2019.

UNECE, 'Report of the First Meeting of the Parties, Decision I/7: Review of Compliance', UN Doc ECE/MP.PP/2/Add.8 (2004).

United Nations Environment Programme (UNEP), 'Guidelines for the Development of Domestic Legislation of Liability, Response Action and Compensation for Damage Cause by Activities Dangerous to the Environment', Governing Council of UNEP, Decision SS.XI/5, Part B (26 February 2010).

United Nations Office for West Africa, 'Communiqué Adopted at the Thirty Second Session of the Cameroon-Nigeria Mixed Commission Established pursuant to the Geneva Joint Communiqué of 15 November 2002', Abuja, 2 February 2014, available at http://unowa.unmissions.org/sites/default/files/Communique%2032MC%20Feb14%20English%20FINAL.pdf, accessed 29 January 2019.

Veeder, V. V., '*Methanex Corporation v. United States of America*, Letter from Tribunal (on Documents Relied upon by Methanex Experts)' (10 October 2003).

von Wobeser, C., *'The Arbitral Tribunal-Appointed Expert'*, in A. J. van den Berg (ed.), *International Arbitration 2006: Back to Basics?*, ICCA Congress Series, 2006 Montreal Volume 13 (Alphen aan den Rijn: Kluwer Law International, 2007) 801–812.

Waincymer, J., *Procedure and Evidence in International Arbitration* (Alphen aan den Rijn: Kluwer Law International, 2012).

Young, M., & J. Muller (eds.), *Knowledge, Expertise and the Professions* (Abingdon: Routledge, 2014).

Cases

Abyei Arbitration (*Sudan v. The Sudan People's Liberation Movement/Army*), Award [2009] ICGJ 422 (Permanent Court of Arbitration).

Argentine-Chile Frontier Case (1966) XVI UNRIAA 109.

Award of the Arbitrator, the President of the United States, upon the validity of the Treaty of Limits of 1858 between Nicaragua and Costa Rica, Papers relating to the Foreign Relations of the United States, 3 December 1888, 456 (U.S. Government Printing Office, 1889).

ICSID, *Bayview Irrigation District et al. v. United Mexican States* [2007] ICSID Case No. ARB/AF/051 (19 June 2007).

ICSID, *Bear Creek Mining Corporation v. Republic of Peru* [2017] ICSID Case No. ARB/14/2 (30 November 2017).

Certain Activities Carried Out by Nicaragua in the Border Area (*Costa Rica v. Nicaragua*) *and Construction of a Road in Costa Rica along the San Juan River* (*Nicaragua v. Costa Rica*), Judgment, ICJ Reports 2015, 665.

Certain Activities Carried Out by Nicaragua in the Border Area (*Costa Rica v. Nicaragua*) *and Construction of a Road in Costa Rica along the San Juan River* (*Nicaragua v. Costa Rica*), Verbatim Record 2015/2.

Certain Activities Carried Out by Nicaragua in the Border Area (*Costa Rica v. Nicaragua*) *and Construction of a Road in Costa Rica along the San Juan River* (*Nicaragua v. Costa Rica*), Verbatim Record 2015/3.

Certain Activities Carried out by Nicaragua in the Border Area (*Costa Rica v. Nicaragua*), *Compensation Owed by the Republic of Nicaragua to the Republic of Costa Rica*, 2 February 2018, ICJ General List No. 150.

Chevron Corporation and Texaco Petroleum Company v. Republic of Ecuador (*Second Partial Award on Track II*) (30 August 2018) PCA Case No. 2009–23.

Corfu Channel (*United Kingdom v. Albania*), Order of 17 December 1948, ICJ Reports 1948, 124.

Corfu Channel (*United Kingdom v. Albania*), Order of 19 November 1949, ICJ Reports 1949, 237.

Delimitation of the Maritime Boundary in the Gulf of Maine Area (*Canada/United States of America*), Judgment, ICJ Reports 1984, 246.

Detroit International Bridge Company v. The Government of Canada (*Award on Jurisdiction*) (2 April 2015) PCA Case No. 2012–25.

Dispute regarding Navigational and Related Rights (*Costa Rica v. Nicaragua*), Judgment, ICJ Reports 2009, 213.

ICSID, *EDF* (*Services*) *Limited v. Romania*, ICSID Case No. ARB/05/13 (8 October 2009).

ICSID, *Fraport AG Frankfurt Airport Services Worldwide v. The Republic of the Philippines* ICSID Case No. ARB/03/25 (16 August 2007).

Frontier Dispute (*Benin/Niger*), ICJ Reports 2005, 90.

Frontier Dispute (Burkina Faso/Niger), Judgment, ICJ Reports 2013, 44.

Frontier Dispute (Burkina Faso/Niger), Order of 12 July 2013, ICJ Reports 2013, 226.

Gabčíkovo-Nagymaros Project (Hungary/Slovakia), Judgment, ICJ Reports 1997, 7.

Gabčíkovo-Nagymaros Project (Hungary/Slovakia), Judgment, Dissenting Opinion of Judge Herczegh, ICJ Reports 1997, 176.

Gabčíkovo-Nagymaros Project (Hungary/Slovakia), Public sitting held on Tuesday 4 March 1997, Verbatim Record 1997/3.

Gut Dam Arbitration [1968] 4 *ILM* 118 (1969).

Indus Waters Kishenganga Arbitration (Pakistan v. India), Final Award [2013] ICGJ 478 (Permanent Court of Arbitration).

Indus Waters Kishenganga Arbitration (Pakistan v. India), Partial Award [2013] ICGJ 476 (Permanent Court of Arbitration).

Kasikili/Sedudu Island (Botswana/Namibia), Merits, Dissenting Opinion of Vice-President Weeramantry, ICJ Reports 1999, 1153.

Kasikili/Sedudu Island (Botswana/Namibia), Merits, Judgment, ICJ Reports 1999, 1045.

Kasikili/Sedudu Island (Botswana/Namibia), Merits, Separate Opinion of Judge Oda, ICJ Reports 1999, 1116.

ICSID, *Kiliç v. Turkmenistan*, Award, ICSID Case No. ARB/10/1 (2 July 2013).

Lake Lanoux Arbitration (Spain/France) (1957) XII UNRIAA 281.

Land and Maritime Boundary between Cameroon and Nigeria (Cameroon v. Nigeria: Equatorial Guinea intervening), Judgment, ICJ Reports 2002, 303.

ICSID, *LG & E Capital Corp and LG & E International Inc v. Argentine Republic*, ICSID Case No. ARB/02/1 (25 July 2007).

Methanex Corporation v. United States of America, Decision of the Tribunal on Petitions from Third Persons to Intervene as '*Amici Curiae*' (UNCITRAL).

Methanex Corporation v. United States of America, Final Award on Jurisdiction and Merits (2005) 44 *ILM* 1345 (UNCITRAL).

Methanex Corporation v. United States of America, Partial Award (Preliminary Award on Jurisdiction and Admissibility) (UNCITRAL).

Methanex Corporation v. United States of America, Rejoinder of USA.

ICSID, *Murphy Exploration and Production Company International v. Republic of Ecuador*, ICSID Case No. ARB/08/4 (15 December 2010).

Obligation to Negotiate Access to the Pacific Ocean (Bolivia v. Chile), Merits, Judgment, 1 October 2018, ICJ General List No. 153.

ICSID, *Occidental Petroleum Corporation and Occidental Exploration and Production Company v. Republic of Ecuador*, ICSID Case No. ARB/06/11 (5 October 2012).

Pulp Mills on the River Uruguay (Argentina v. Uruguay), Judgment, ICJ Reports 2010, 14.

Pulp Mills on the River Uruguay (Argentina v. Uruguay), Judgment, Declaration of Judge Yusuf, ICJ Reports 2010, 216.

Pulp Mills on the River Uruguay (Argentina v. Uruguay), Judgment, Dissenting Opinion of Judge ad hoc Vinuesa, ICJ Reports 2010, 266.

Pulp Mills on the River Uruguay (Argentina v. Uruguay), Judgment, Joint Dissenting Opinion of Judges Al Khasawneh and Simma, ICJ Reports 2010, 108.

Pulp Mills on the River Uruguay (Argentina v. Uruguay), Judgment, Separate Opinion of Judge Keith, ICJ Reports 2010, 121.

Rhine Chlorides Arbitration Concerning the Auditing of Accounts (The Netherlands/France) (11 March 2004) PCA Case No. 2000–02.

Ruling concerning the disagreement between Ecuador and Peru over the Zamora-Santiago Sector (1945) XXVIII UNRIAA 413.

ICSID, *Salini Costruttori S.pA and Italstrade S.pA v. Hashemite Kingdom of Jordan*, ICSID Case No. ARB/02/13 (31 January 2006).

Sergei Paushok, CJSC Golden East Company and CJSC Vostokneftegaz Company v. The Government of Mongolia (28 April 2011) UNCITRAL Arbitration, available at http://www.italaw.com/sites/default/files/case-documents/ita0622.pdf, accessed 31 January 2019.

ICSID, *SGS Société Générale de Surveillance S A v. The Republic of Paraguay*, ICSID Case No. ARB/07/29 (10 February 2012).

Tacna–Arica Question (Chile/Peru) (1925) II UNRIAA 921.

The Chamizal Case (Mexico/United States) (1911) XI UNRIAA 309.

Trail Smelter Arbitration (United States v. Canada) (1941) 3 UNRIAA 1905.

United States District Court, *Anderson v. American Smelting & Refining Co.*, 265 Federal Reporter 928 (Judge Johnson).

Vattenfall AB, Vattenfall Europe AG, Vattenfall Europe Generation AG v Federal Republic of Germany ICSID Case No. ARB/09/6 (11 March 2011).

Western Sahara, Advisory Opinion, Separate Opinion of Judge Petrén, ICJ Reports 1975, 104.

Whaling in the Antarctic (Australia v. Japan: New Zealand intervening), Judgment, ICJ Reports 2014, 226.

Treaties, Statutes and Rules

Conference of the Parties to the Convention on Biological Diversity, Decision XII/14 (2014).

Convention between the United States of America and the United States of Mexico Touching the International Boundary Line where it follows the Bed of the Rio Grande and the Rio Colorado, 12 November 1884, 1884, 24 Stat 1011; Treaty Series 226.

Convention for the Settlement of Investment Disputes Between States and Nationals of Other States, 18 March 1965, entered into force 14 October 1966, 575 *UNTS* 159.

Convention on Access to Information, Public Participation in Decision-Making and Access to Justice in Environmental Matters, 25 June 1998, entered into force 30 October 2001, 2161 *UNTS* 447.

Convention on the Law of the Non-Navigational Uses of International Watercourses, 21 May 1997, entered into force 17 August 2014, 36 *ILM* 700 (1997).

Convention on the Protection and Use of Transboundary Watercourses and International Lakes, 17 March 1992, entered into force 6 October 1996, 1936 *UNTS* 269.

Franco-British Declaration (Milner-Simon Declaration), LON/BPC/MAN/75 (1919).

Helgoland–Zanzibar Treaty (Anglo-German Agreement), 1 July 1890, available at http://germanhistorydocs.ghi-dc.org/pdf/eng/606_Anglo-German%20Treaty_110.pdf; accessed 19 July 2019.

ICSID Arbitration (Additional Facility) Rules 2006 (ICSID/11 (2006)).

ICSID Rules of Procedure for Arbitration Proceedings 2006 (ICSID/15 (2006)).

Indus Waters Treaty between the Government of India, the Government of Pakistan and the International Bank for Reconstruction and Development, 19 September 1960, 419 *UNTS* 125.

International Bar Association Guidelines on Party Representation in International Arbitration 2013, available at http://www.ibanet.org/Document/Default.aspx?DocumentUid=6F0C57D7-E7A0-43AF-B76E-714D9FE74D7F; accessed 20 June 2019.

International Bar Association Rules on the Taking of Evidence in International Arbitration 2010, available at http://www.ibanet.org/Document/Default.aspx?DocumentUid=68336C49-4106-46BF-A1C6-A8F0880444DC; accessed 20 June 2019.

International Law Commission, Model Rules on Arbitral Procedure 1958, *Yearbook of the International Law Commission, 1958*, vol. II.

North American Free Trade Agreement, 17 December 1992, entered into force 1 January 1994, 32 *ILM* 289, 605 (1993).

Permanent Court of Arbitration Optional Rules for Arbitrating Disputes between Two Parties of Which Only One is a State (1993) available at http://pca-cpa.org/wp-content/uploads/sites/6/2016/01/Optional-Rules-for-Arbitrating-Disputes-between-Two-Parties-of-Which-Only-One-is-a-State-1993.pdf; accessed 17 July 2019.

Permanent Court of Arbitration Optional Rules for Arbitration of Disputes relating to Natural Resources and/or the Environment (2012) available at http://pca-cpa.org/wp-content/uploads/sites/175/2016/01/Optional-Rules-for-Arbitration-of-Disputes-Relating-to-the-Environment-and_or-Natural-Resources.pdf; accessed 1 November 2016.

Permanent Court of Arbitration Optional Rules for Fact-Finding Commissions of Inquiry (2012) available at http://pca-cpa.org/wp-content/uploads/sites/6/2016/01/Permanent-Court-of-Arbitration-Optional-Rules-for-Fact-finding-Commissions-of-Inquiry.pdf; accessed 1 November 2016.

Permanent Court of Arbitration Arbitration Rules (2012) available at http://pca-cpa.org/wp-content/uploads/sites/6/2015/11/PCA-Arbitration-Rules-2012.pdf; accessed 1 November 2016.

Protocol of Peace, Friendship, and Boundaries between Peru and Ecuador (Rio Protocol) 29 January 1942 ((1942) 36 AJIL 168).

Protocol on Pollutant Release and Transfer Registers to the Convention on Access to Information, Public Participation in Decision-Making and Access to Justice in Environmental Matters, 21 May 2003, entered into force 8 October 2009, 2626 *UNTS* 119.

Protocol on Water and Health to the 1992 Convention on the Protection and Use of Transboundary Watercourses and International Lakes, 17 June 1999, entered into force 4 August 2005, 2331 *UNTS* 202.

R. Lafitte, Baglihar Hydroelectric Plant, Expert Determination on points of difference referred by the Government of Pakistan under the provisions of the Indus Waters Treaty, Executive Summary, Lausanne, 12 February 2007, available at http://siteresources.worldbank.org/SOUTHASIAEXT/Resources/223546-1171996340255/BagliharSummary.pdf.

International Court of Justice, Rules of Court 1946, Acts and Documents Concerning the Organization of the Court (2nd edition, 1947).

International Court of Justice, Rules of Court 1972, Acts and Documents Concerning the Organization of the Court, No. 2 (Sales No. 364).

International Court of Justice, Rules of Court, 14 April 1978, entered into forced 1 July 1978, as amended in 2005 *Acts and Documents No. 6* (2007).

United Nations, Statute of the International Court of Justice, 26 June 1945, entered into force 24 October 1945, 3 Bevans 1179.

Treaty Concerning the Construction and Operation of the Gabčíkovo-Nagymaros System of Locks, 16 September 1977, 1109 *UNTS* 211.

Treaty of Peace between Chile and Peru (Treaty of Ancón), 20 October 1883 (Peru, Ministerio de Relaciones Exteriores (1936) *Tratados, convenciones y acuerdosvigentes entre el Perú y otros estados I*, Lima: Imprenta Torres Aguirre: 165–168).

Treaty of Peace, Friendship, Limits and Settlement between the United States of America and the Mexican Republic (Treaty of Guadalupe Hidalgo), 2 February 1848, 9 Bevans 791.

Treaty of Territorial Limits between Costa Rica and Nicaragua (Cañas-Jerez Treaty), 15 April 1858, available at http://www.manfut.org/cronologia/jerez.html; accessed 19 July 2019.

Treaty on boundaries between Spain and France from the valley of Andorra to the Mediterranean (with additional act) (Treaty of Bayonne), 26 May 1866, 1288 *UNTS* 305.

United Nations Commission on International Trade Law (UNCITRAL), UNCITRAL Arbitration Rules 2013, UN Doc A/RES/68/109 (16 December 2013).

www.ingramcontent.com/pod-product-compliance
Lightning Source LLC
Chambersburg PA
CBHW031330230926
51848CB00001B/167